What Could Possibly Go Wrong?

Also by Dave Walker and available from Canterbury Press

The Dave Walker Colouring Book

Heroes of the Coffee Rota

Peculiar Goings On

The Exciting World of Church Going

The Dave Walker Guide to the Church

My Pew: Things I Have Seen from It

How to Avoid the Peace

The Revenge of the Flower Arrangers

www.canterburypress.co.uk

What Could Possibly Go Wrong?

Dave Walker

CANTERBURY
PRESS
Norwich

© Dave Walker 2021

First published in 2021 by the Canterbury Press Norwich
Editorial office
3rd Floor, Invicta House
108–114 Golden Lane
London EC1Y 0TG, UK
www.canterburypress.co.uk

Canterbury Press is an imprint of Hymns Ancient & Modern Ltd (a registered charity)

Hymns Ancient & Modern® is a registered trademark of Hymns Ancient & Modern Ltd
13A Hellesdon Park Road, Norwich,
Norfolk NR6 5DR, UK

British Library Cataloguing in Publication data

A catalogue record for this book is available
from the British Library

ISBN 978-1-78622-409-5

Printed and bound in Great Britain by
CPI Group (UK) Ltd

Contents

Part 3 The Church Year, Looking Forward 71

Introduction

This is, if I've done my sums correctly, the eighth book of my cartoons for the *Church Times*. Each cartoon represents a deadline day wrestling with an idea that somehow more-or-less comes together approximately in time for the time it needs to be sent. It's a great privilege to be able to draw something for the paper every week, and I hope you enjoy this collection.

Under normal circumstances the order of the cartoons in the books is decided by a complex algorithm that only I understand. But, as an exciting innovation, this book is divided into three parts. Part One, 'People, Buildings, Controversies', contains various drawings from before the pandemic. Part Two contains a selection of cartoons from 2020, many drawn during lockdown, entitled 'The Pandemic'. And then, to end on an uplifting note (and/or to find a home for the diagrams that didn't fit anywhere else), we conclude with Part Three, 'The Church Year, Looking Forward'.

I'd like to thank everyone who supports my work and makes it possible. First of all everyone who sends me material, and those who may or may not belong to my highly secret ideas-gathering group (if such a thing exists). A particular thank you to Jayne Manfredi, who wrote the wonderful words to 'Beatitudes for a Global Pandemic', the cartoon that summed up 2020 in a more complete way than anything I could have managed on my own. Most especially I'd like to thank Charlotte, my wife, who contributes to my cartooning endeavours in numerous ways, not least by helping me refine my more mediocre ideas, and putting up with my low morale during the drawing process. And to everyone who encourages, likes, shares, retweets and comments kindly – thank you.

Dave
Langdon Hills, May 2021

Website: CartoonChurch.com
Twitter: @davewalker

PART ONE: PEOPLE, BUILDINGS, CONTROVERSIES

ALLOCATED DUTIES

THEY ARE NOT READILY RELINQUISHED

KEEP OUT
KITCHEN
TRAINED USERS ONLY
RULES
NO
FORBIDDING NOTICES

KENNETH ARRANGES THE CUPS AND SAUCERS

DECOY KEY CABINET
KEYS

MARGARET OPENS THE SOUTH DOOR

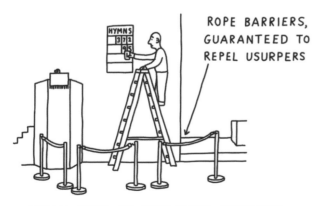

HYMNS
ROPE BARRIERS, GUARANTEED TO REPEL USURPERS

BRIAN PUTS UP THE HYMN NUMBERS

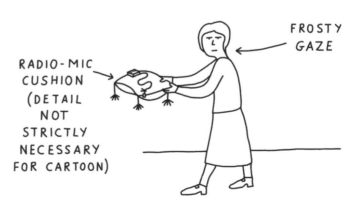

FROSTY GAZE
RADIO-MIC CUSHION (DETAIL NOT STRICTLY NECESSARY FOR CARTOON)

DOREEN DELIVERS THE RADIO MICROPHONE

FLOWER ARRANGING

THINGS YOU WILL NEED

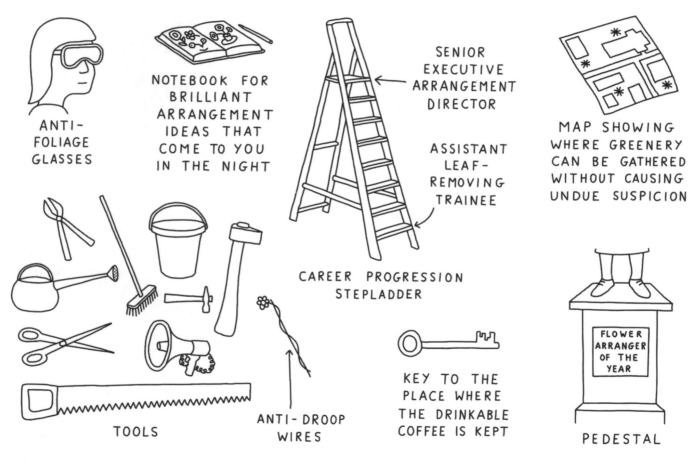

ANTI-FOLIAGE GLASSES

NOTEBOOK FOR BRILLIANT ARRANGEMENT IDEAS THAT COME TO YOU IN THE NIGHT

SENIOR EXECUTIVE ARRANGEMENT DIRECTOR

ASSISTANT LEAF-REMOVING TRAINEE

CAREER PROGRESSION STEPLADDER

MAP SHOWING WHERE GREENERY CAN BE GATHERED WITHOUT CAUSING UNDUE SUSPICION

TOOLS

ANTI-DROOP WIRES

KEY TO THE PLACE WHERE THE DRINKABLE COFFEE IS KEPT

FLOWER ARRANGER OF THE YEAR

PEDESTAL

THE FLOWER ARRANGERS

WHAT ARE THEY TRYING TO HIDE?

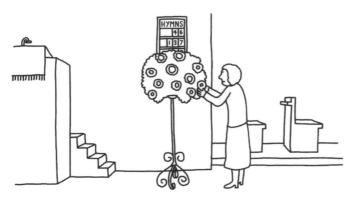

AN OVERUSED HYMN

AN UNINSPIRING PREACHER

A SECRET LAIR

A WINDOW THEY BROKE ON FRIDAY

THE RINGING CHAMBER

HOME OF THE BELL RINGERS

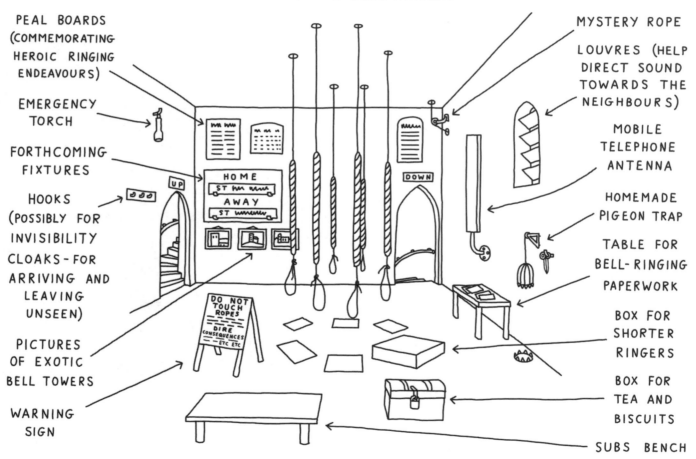

PEAL BOARDS (COMMEMORATING HEROIC RINGING ENDEAVOURS)

EMERGENCY TORCH

FORTHCOMING FIXTURES

HOOKS (POSSIBLY FOR INVISIBILITY CLOAKS - FOR ARRIVING AND LEAVING UNSEEN)

PICTURES OF EXOTIC BELL TOWERS

WARNING SIGN

MYSTERY ROPE

LOUVRES (HELP DIRECT SOUND TOWARDS THE NEIGHBOURS)

MOBILE TELEPHONE ANTENNA

HOMEMADE PIGEON TRAP

TABLE FOR BELL-RINGING PAPERWORK

BOX FOR SHORTER RINGERS

BOX FOR TEA AND BISCUITS

SUBS BENCH

UP

HOME
ST
AWAY
ST

DOWN

DO NOT TOUCH ROPES
DIRE CONSEQUENCES
ETC ETC

6

SERVERS

THEIR RESPONSIBILITIES

PROCESSING SYMMETRICALLY

400 YEAR-OLD MARIGOLDS →

WASHING UP THE 400 YEAR-OLD SILVERWARE

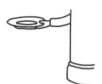

MERGING INTO THE BACKGROUND, AS NECESSARY

PUTTING ON A ROBE SUCCESSFULLY

GUARDING THE COLLECTION

AVOIDING OBSTACLES

OH — AND A GARLIC BREAD

FETCHING AND CARRYING THINGS AS REQUIRED

ACTING IN A CONTROLLED AND DIGNIFIED FASHION IN ALL CIRCUMSTANCES

7

PROCESSION SCHOOL
THE THINGS YOU WILL LEARN

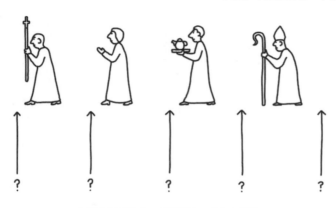

KNOWING YOUR PLACE

SPIN ON BALL OF FOOT AT THIS POINT

HOW TO TURN A CORNER

WHAT TO DO WITH YOUR HANDS

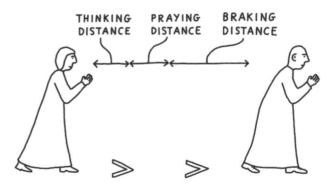

THINKING DISTANCE   PRAYING DISTANCE   BRAKING DISTANCE

SAFE STOPPING DISTANCES

CHURCHWARDENS

HOW TO RECOGNISE THEM IN A DOMESTIC SETTING

DO WE NEED A FACULTY FOR THIS?

GOOD WITH PRACTICALITIES

CHOC

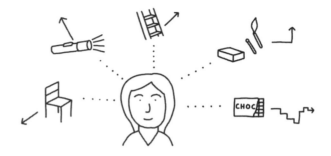

ABLE TO LOCATE ANYTHING AT A MOMENT'S NOTICE

THIS CURTAIN'S LOOKING A LITTLE WORN...

TAKING RESPONSIBILITY FOR THE FABRIC OF THE BUILDING

CARRYING A MULTITUDE OF KEYS

SIDESPERSONS

COMMON MISUNDERSTANDINGS ABOUT THEIR ROLE

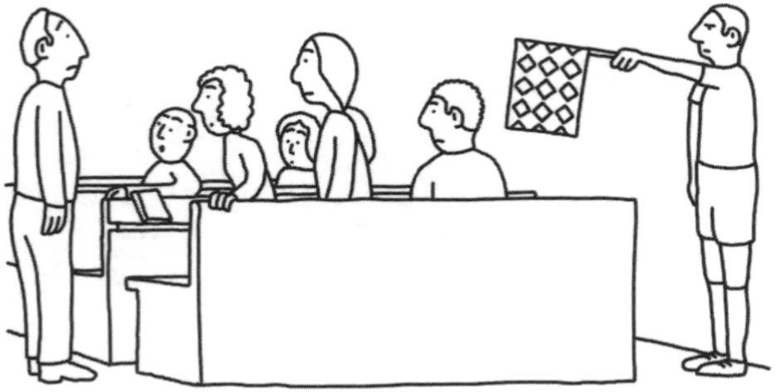

PEOPLE WHO KEEP AN EYE ON THINGS FROM THE SIDE AISLES

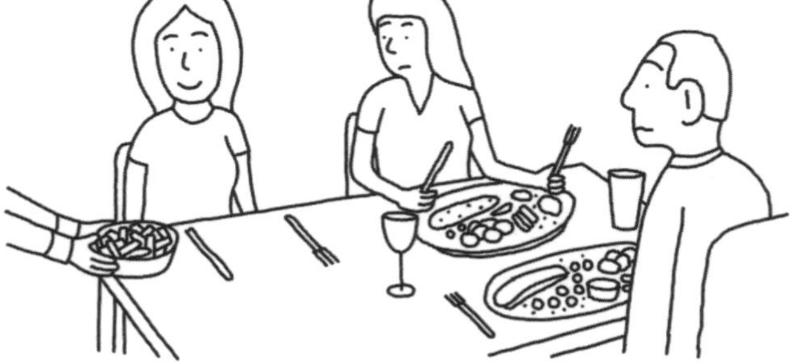

FRIENDS WHO ONLY ORDER CHIPS AT A RESTAURANT

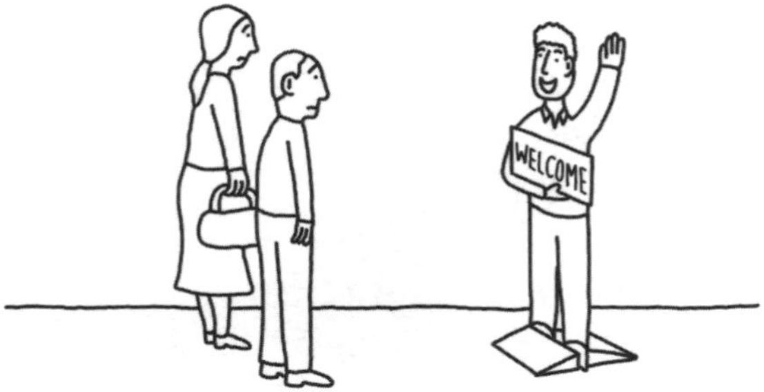
WELCOME

PERSONS MADE UP ONLY OF SIDES

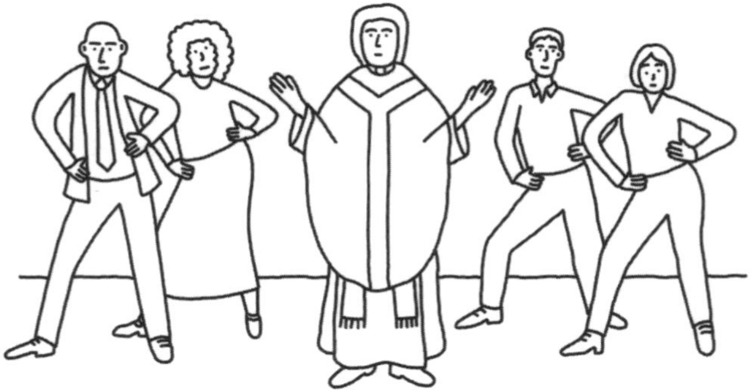

BACKING DANCERS FOR LITURGICAL ROUTINES

THE MEMORY STICK

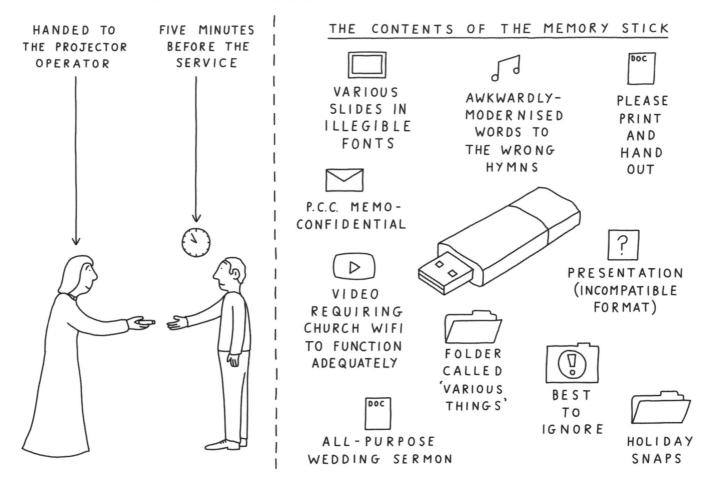

HANDED TO
THE PROJECTOR
OPERATOR

FIVE MINUTES
BEFORE THE
SERVICE

THE CONTENTS OF THE MEMORY STICK

VARIOUS
SLIDES IN
ILLEGIBLE
FONTS

AWKWARDLY-
MODERNISED
WORDS TO
THE WRONG
HYMNS

PLEASE
PRINT
AND
HAND
OUT

P.C.C. MEMO-
CONFIDENTIAL

VIDEO
REQUIRING
CHURCH WIFI
TO FUNCTION
ADEQUATELY

FOLDER
CALLED
'VARIOUS
THINGS'

PRESENTATION
(INCOMPATIBLE
FORMAT)

BEST
TO
IGNORE

HOLIDAY
SNAPS

ALL-PURPOSE
WEDDING SERMON

THE SOUND SYSTEM

HOW TO STOP THAT TERRIBLE FEEDBACK SOUND

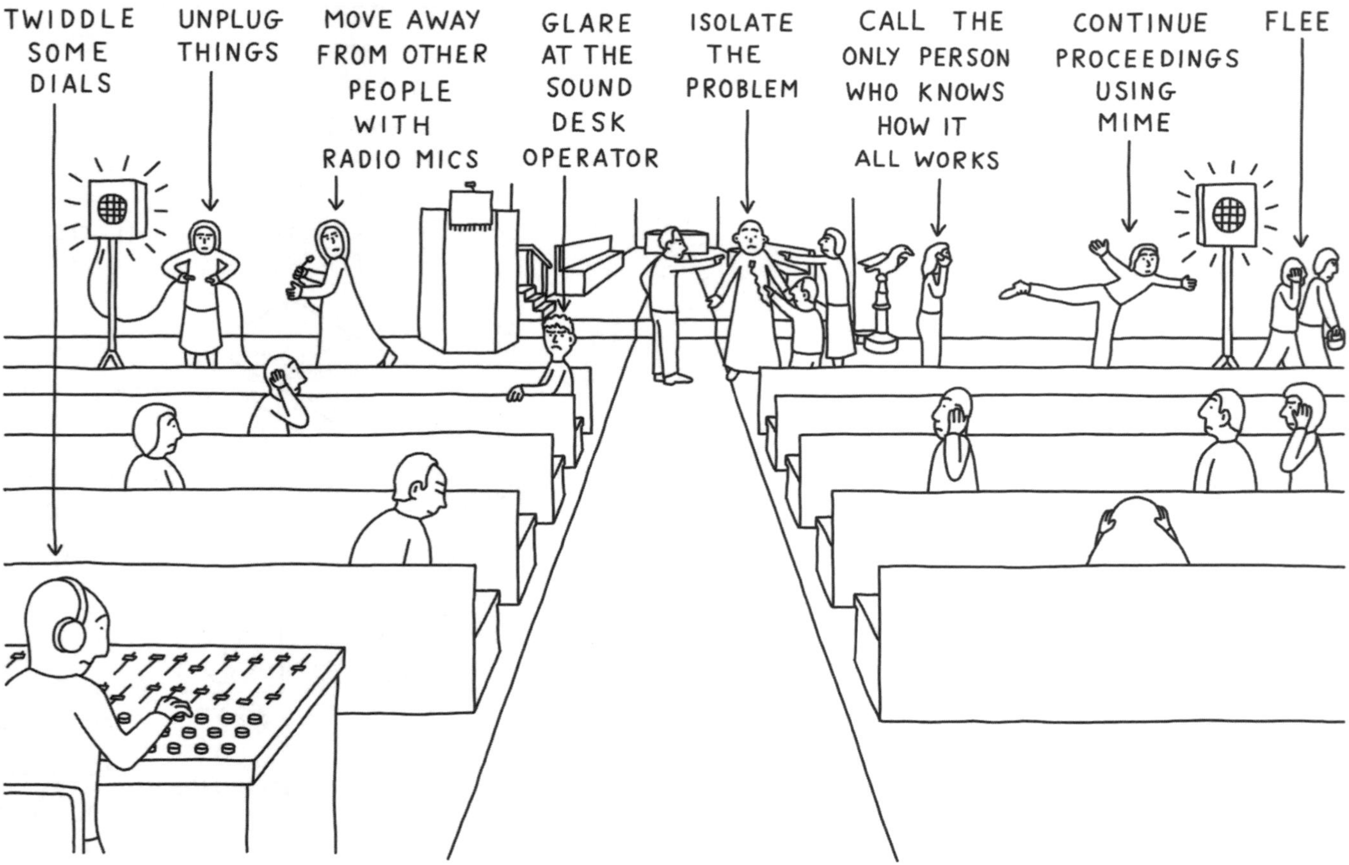
TWIDDLE SOME DIALS
UNPLUG THINGS
MOVE AWAY FROM OTHER PEOPLE WITH RADIO MICS
GLARE AT THE SOUND DESK OPERATOR
ISOLATE THE PROBLEM
CALL THE ONLY PERSON WHO KNOWS HOW IT ALL WORKS
CONTINUE PROCEEDINGS USING MIME
FLEE

COUNTING THE COLLECTION

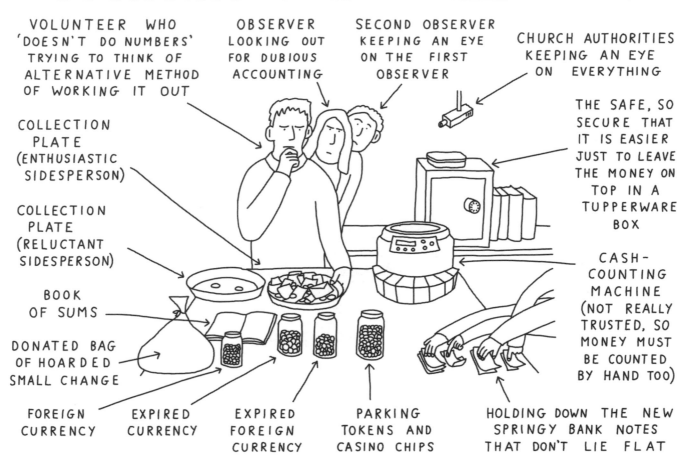

VOLUNTEER WHO 'DOESN'T DO NUMBERS' TRYING TO THINK OF ALTERNATIVE METHOD OF WORKING IT OUT

OBSERVER LOOKING OUT FOR DUBIOUS ACCOUNTING

SECOND OBSERVER KEEPING AN EYE ON THE FIRST OBSERVER

CHURCH AUTHORITIES KEEPING AN EYE ON EVERYTHING

COLLECTION PLATE (ENTHUSIASTIC SIDESPERSON)

THE SAFE, SO SECURE THAT IT IS EASIER JUST TO LEAVE THE MONEY ON TOP IN A TUPPERWARE BOX

COLLECTION PLATE (RELUCTANT SIDESPERSON)

BOOK OF SUMS

CASH-COUNTING MACHINE (NOT REALLY TRUSTED, SO MONEY MUST BE COUNTED BY HAND TOO)

DONATED BAG OF HOARDED SMALL CHANGE

FOREIGN CURRENCY

EXPIRED CURRENCY

EXPIRED FOREIGN CURRENCY

PARKING TOKENS AND CASINO CHIPS

HOLDING DOWN THE NEW SPRINGY BANK NOTES THAT DON'T LIE FLAT

REFRESHMENTS
EMERGENCY PROCEDURES

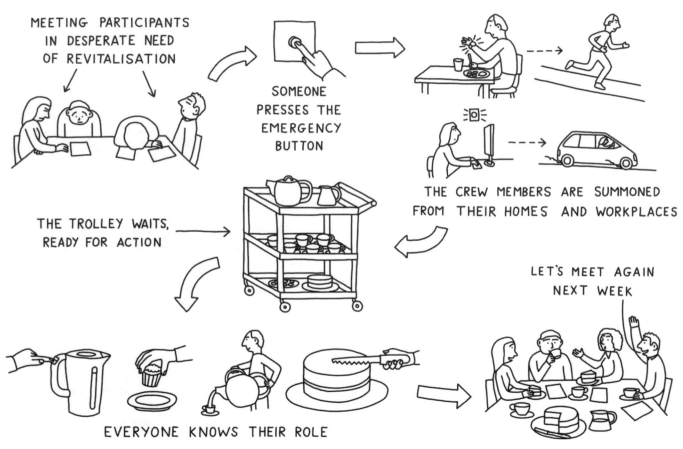

MEETING PARTICIPANTS IN DESPERATE NEED OF REVITALISATION

SOMEONE PRESSES THE EMERGENCY BUTTON

THE CREW MEMBERS ARE SUMMONED FROM THEIR HOMES AND WORKPLACES

THE TROLLEY WAITS, READY FOR ACTION

EVERYONE KNOWS THEIR ROLE

LET'S MEET AGAIN NEXT WEEK

THE RURAL CHURCH

WHAT TO EXPECT DURING YOUR FIRST MONTH

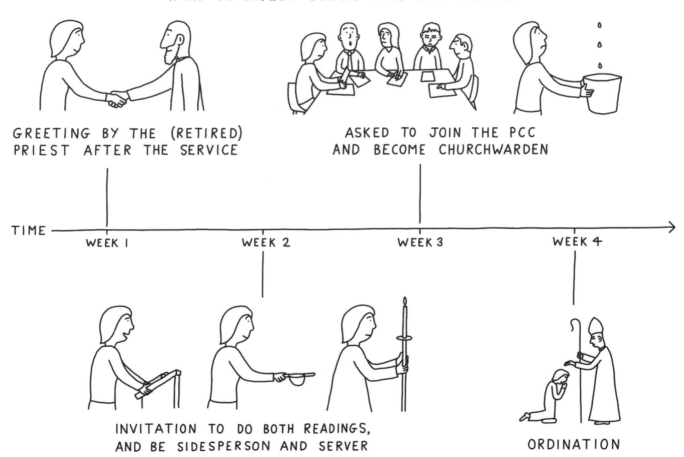

GREETING BY THE (RETIRED)
PRIEST AFTER THE SERVICE

ASKED TO JOIN THE PCC
AND BECOME CHURCHWARDEN

TIME

WEEK 1   WEEK 2   WEEK 3   WEEK 4

INVITATION TO DO BOTH READINGS,
AND BE SIDESPERSON AND SERVER

ORDINATION

UNDERCOVER CLERGY

CHARACTERISTICS OF POTENTIAL NEW VICARS VISITING UNANNOUNCED DURING A VACANCY

TRYING TO BLEND IN

LOITERING NEAR THE VICARAGE

KNOWING A BIT MORE OF THE LITURGY THAN IS NORMAL

VESTRY
COLLECTION COUNTING IN PROGRESS

TAKING AN UNUSUAL INTEREST IN THE STATE OF THE FINANCES

SO, ARE YOU VISITING?
YES... I MEAN... NO...

APPEARING EVASIVE WHEN ASKED QUESTIONS

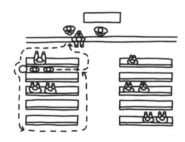

UNDERSTANDING HOW THE COMMUNION ONE-WAY SYSTEM WORKS

0.5 ROLES

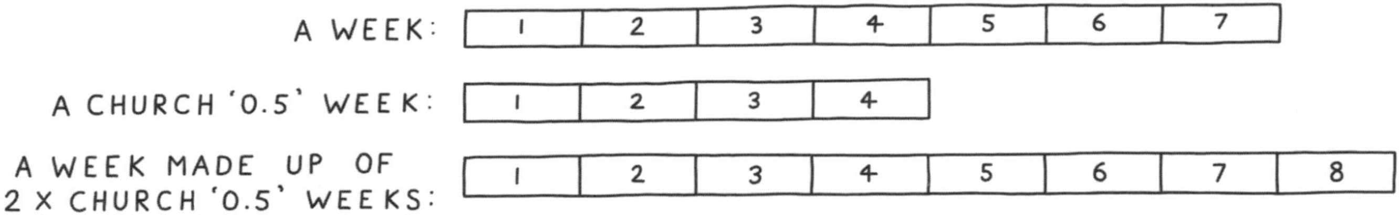

A WEEK:	1	2	3	4	5	6	7	

A CHURCH '0.5' WEEK:	1	2	3	4				

A WEEK MADE UP OF 2 X CHURCH '0.5' WEEKS:	1	2	3	4	5	6	7	8

ADVICE FOR PRIESTS FITTING TWO 0.5 ROLES INTO A WEEK

DO BOTH JOBS AT ONCE

USE TECHNOLOGY

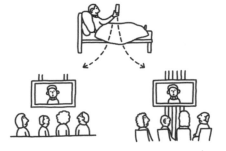

DOUBLES AND DECOYS

WORK LONGER HOURS

PREVIOUS INCUMBENTS

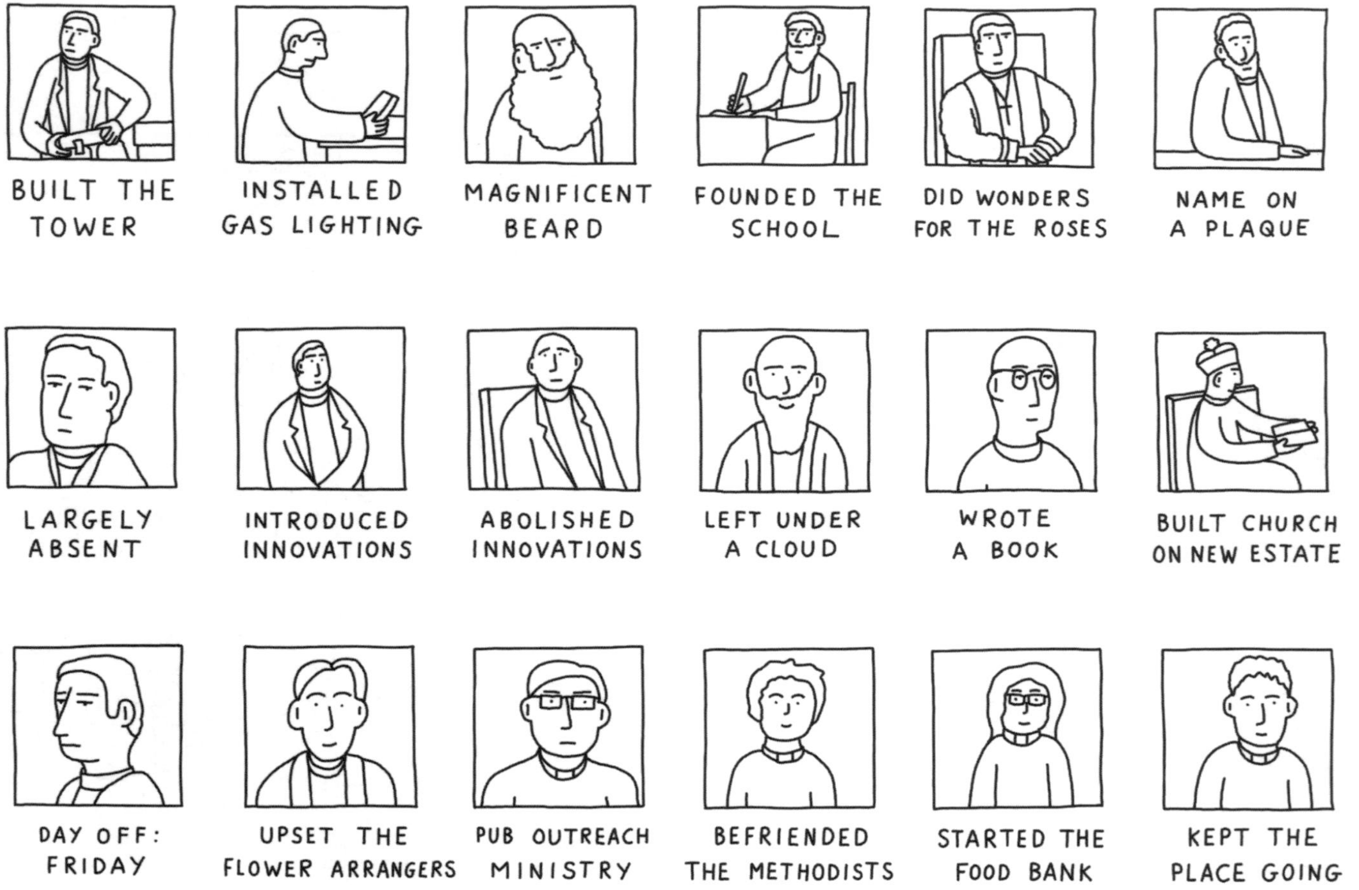
BUILT THE TOWER
INSTALLED GAS LIGHTING
MAGNIFICENT BEARD
FOUNDED THE SCHOOL
DID WONDERS FOR THE ROSES
NAME ON A PLAQUE
LARGELY ABSENT
INTRODUCED INNOVATIONS
ABOLISHED INNOVATIONS
LEFT UNDER A CLOUD
WROTE A BOOK
BUILT CHURCH ON NEW ESTATE
DAY OFF: FRIDAY
UPSET THE FLOWER ARRANGERS
PUB OUTREACH MINISTRY
BEFRIENDED THE METHODISTS
STARTED THE FOOD BANK
KEPT THE PLACE GOING

THE BOOK OF COMMON PRAYER

HOW LONG DOES IT TAKE YOU TO LOCATE A COPY?

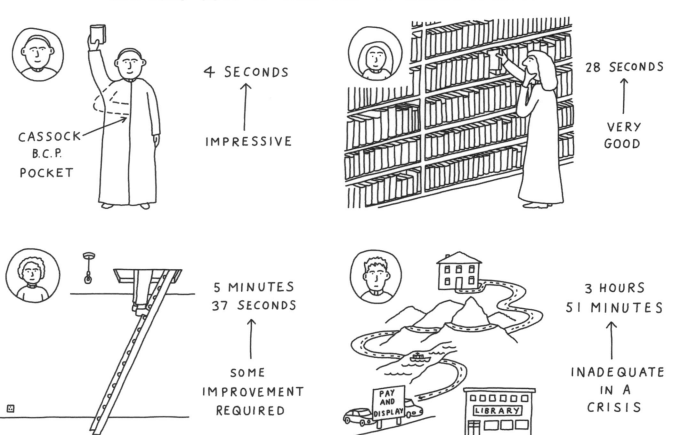

CASSOCK
B.C.P.
POCKET

4 SECONDS

IMPRESSIVE

28 SECONDS

VERY
GOOD

5 MINUTES
37 SECONDS

SOME
IMPROVEMENT
REQUIRED

PAY
AND
DISPLAY

LIBRARY

3 HOURS
51 MINUTES

INADEQUATE
IN A
CRISIS

NEW BISHOPS

TRAVEL THEIR DIOCESES TO VISIT ALL OF THE CHURCHES

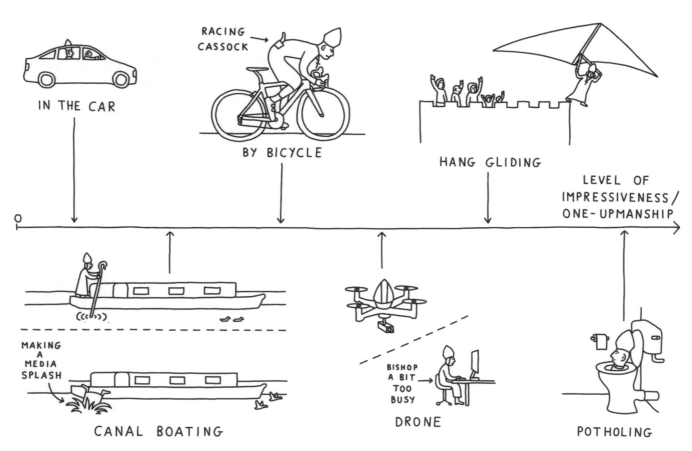

RACING CASSOCK

IN THE CAR

BY BICYCLE

HANG GLIDING

LEVEL OF IMPRESSIVENESS/ ONE-UPMANSHIP

MAKING A MEDIA SPLASH

CANAL BOATING

BISHOP A BIT TOO BUSY

DRONE

POTHOLING

THE PARISH CHURCH

SEEN FROM ABOVE

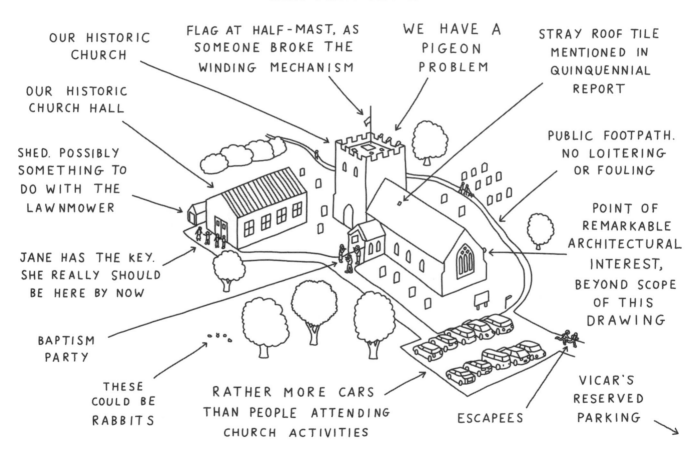

OUR HISTORIC CHURCH

FLAG AT HALF-MAST, AS SOMEONE BROKE THE WINDING MECHANISM

WE HAVE A PIGEON PROBLEM

STRAY ROOF TILE MENTIONED IN QUINQUENNIAL REPORT

OUR HISTORIC CHURCH HALL

SHED. POSSIBLY SOMETHING TO DO WITH THE LAWNMOWER

PUBLIC FOOTPATH. NO LOITERING OR FOULING

POINT OF REMARKABLE ARCHITECTURAL INTEREST, BEYOND SCOPE OF THIS DRAWING

JANE HAS THE KEY. SHE REALLY SHOULD BE HERE BY NOW

BAPTISM PARTY

THESE COULD BE RABBITS

RATHER MORE CARS THAN PEOPLE ATTENDING CHURCH ACTIVITIES

ESCAPEES

VICAR'S RESERVED PARKING

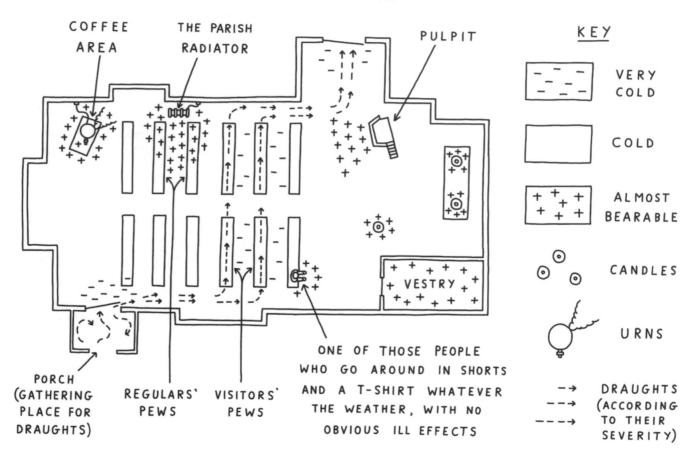

THE CHURCH BUILDING
A HEAT MAP

COFFEE AREA

THE PARISH RADIATOR

PULPIT

KEY

VERY COLD

COLD

ALMOST BEARABLE

CANDLES

URNS

DRAUGHTS (ACCORDING TO THEIR SEVERITY)

PORCH (GATHERING PLACE FOR DRAUGHTS)

REGULARS' PEWS

VISITORS' PEWS

VESTRY

ONE OF THOSE PEOPLE WHO GO AROUND IN SHORTS AND A T-SHIRT WHATEVER THE WEATHER, WITH NO OBVIOUS ILL EFFECTS

THE CHAIRS

WAYS TO ARRANGE THEM

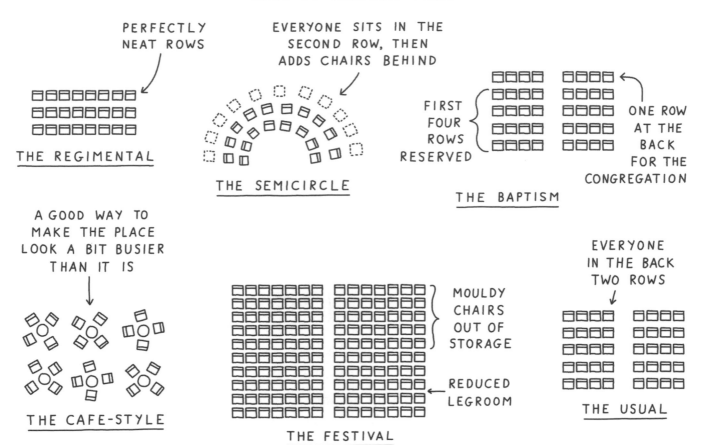

PERFECTLY NEAT ROWS

THE REGIMENTAL

EVERYONE SITS IN THE SECOND ROW, THEN ADDS CHAIRS BEHIND

THE SEMICIRCLE

FIRST FOUR ROWS RESERVED

ONE ROW AT THE BACK FOR THE CONGREGATION

THE BAPTISM

A GOOD WAY TO MAKE THE PLACE LOOK A BIT BUSIER THAN IT IS

THE CAFE-STYLE

MOULDY CHAIRS OUT OF STORAGE

REDUCED LEGROOM

THE FESTIVAL

EVERYONE IN THE BACK TWO ROWS

THE USUAL

FOLDING TABLES

COMMON SCENES

A FLAGRANT DISREGARD FOR THE INSTRUCTION MANUAL

☐ REFERENCES
☐ INSURANCE
☐ BIRTH CERTIFICATE
☐ HOUSEHOLD BILL
☐ TENUOUS CONNECTION TO SOMEONE IN THE CONGREGATION

CHECKLIST FOR THOSE WANTING TO BORROW TABLES

BORROWING
RETURNING

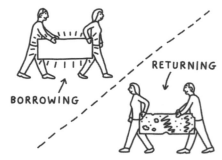

BORROWERS, WHO HAVE NOT BEEN PARTICULARLY DILIGENT

SEMINAR FOR THOSE NEW TO THE UNFOLDING PROCESS

THOSE WHO DO NOT NEED THE SPECIAL TABLE TOOL LOOKING DOWN ON THOSE WHO DO

THE MAN WHO CAN UNFOLD TWO TABLES SIMULTANEOUSLY

THE WIRING DIAGRAM

(APPROXIMATE)

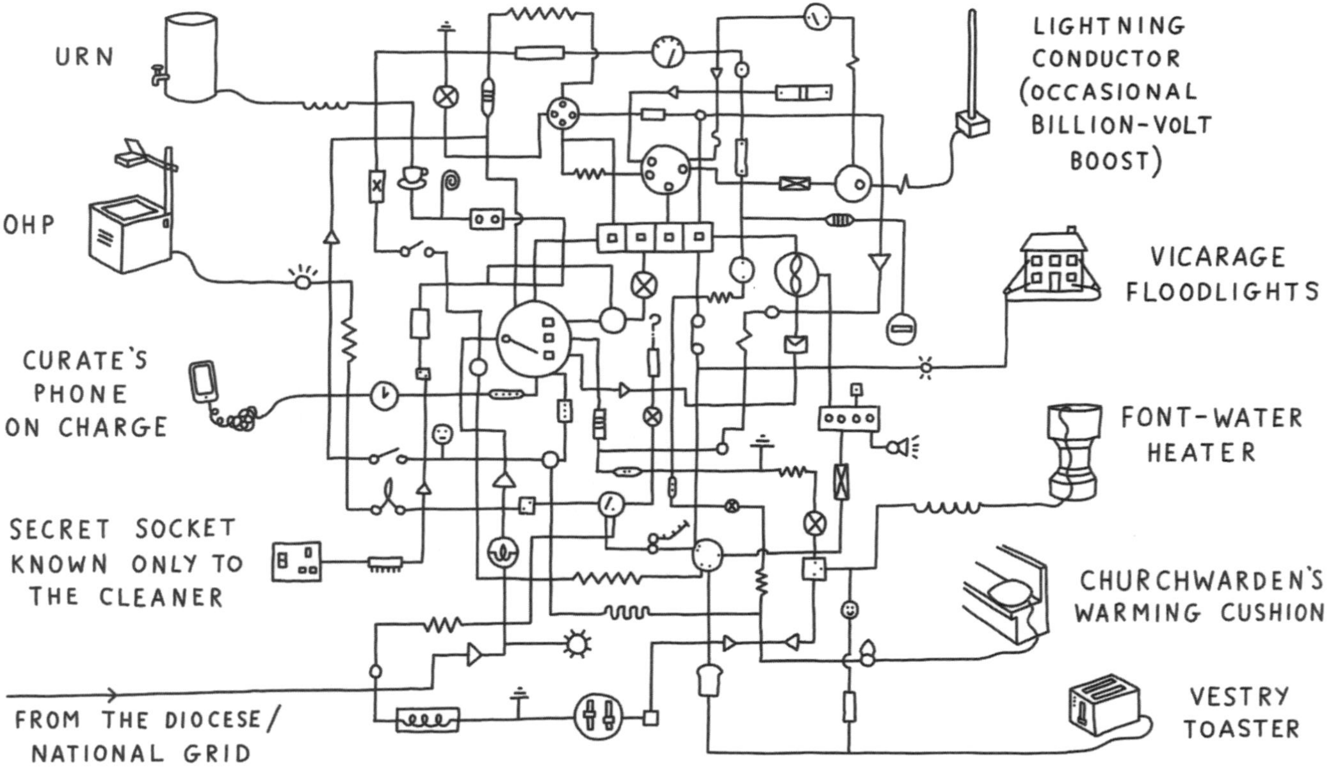

URN
LIGHTNING CONDUCTOR (OCCASIONAL BILLION-VOLT BOOST)
OHP
VICARAGE FLOODLIGHTS
CURATE'S PHONE ON CHARGE
FONT-WATER HEATER
SECRET SOCKET KNOWN ONLY TO THE CLEANER
CHURCHWARDEN'S WARMING CUSHION
VESTRY TOASTER
FROM THE DIOCESE/ NATIONAL GRID

WARNING: DO NOT ATTEMPT TO USE THIS DIAGRAM, EVEN IF ACCOMPANIED BY A COMPETENT PERSON

PERMITTED ACTIVITIES

IN THE CHURCH AND CHURCH HALL

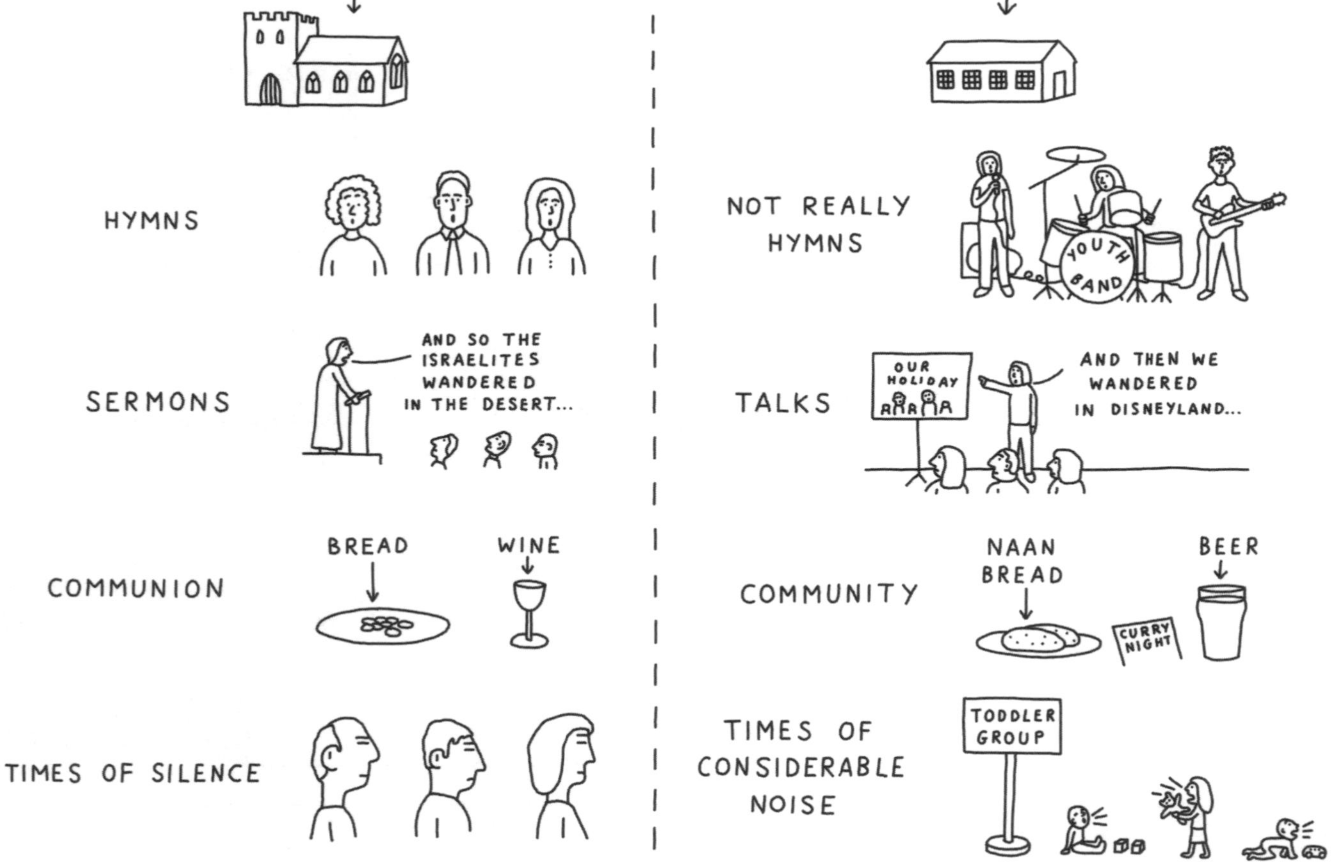
HYMNS
NOT REALLY HYMNS
YOUTH BAND
SERMONS
AND SO THE ISRAELITES WANDERED IN THE DESERT...
TALKS
OUR HOLIDAY
AND THEN WE WANDERED IN DISNEYLAND...
COMMUNION
BREAD
WINE
COMMUNITY
NAAN BREAD
CURRY NIGHT
BEER
TIMES OF SILENCE
TIMES OF CONSIDERABLE NOISE
TODDLER GROUP

THE MEETING ROOM
WHO IS IN THERE?

THE TODDLER GROUP

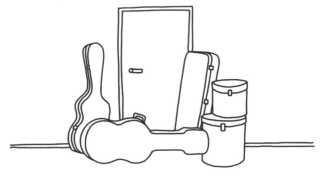

THE MUSIC TEAM

THE AFTER-SCHOOL CLUB

THE BISHOP, MEDIATING BETWEEN THE
FLOWER ARRANGERS AND THE YOUTH GROUP

THE CHURCH FRIDGE

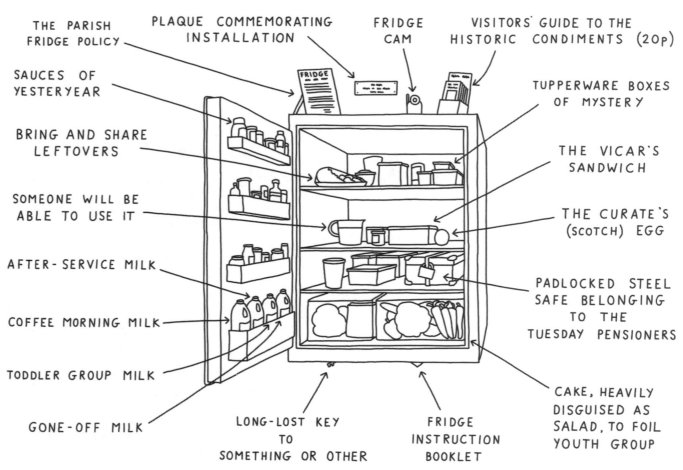

THE PARISH FRIDGE POLICY

PLAQUE COMMEMORATING INSTALLATION

FRIDGE CAM

VISITORS' GUIDE TO THE HISTORIC CONDIMENTS (20p)

SAUCES OF YESTERYEAR

TUPPERWARE BOXES OF MYSTERY

BRING AND SHARE LEFTOVERS

THE VICAR'S SANDWICH

SOMEONE WILL BE ABLE TO USE IT

THE CURATE'S (SCOTCH) EGG

AFTER-SERVICE MILK

PADLOCKED STEEL SAFE BELONGING TO THE TUESDAY PENSIONERS

COFFEE MORNING MILK

TODDLER GROUP MILK

GONE-OFF MILK

LONG-LOST KEY TO SOMETHING OR OTHER

FRIDGE INSTRUCTION BOOKLET

CAKE, HEAVILY DISGUISED AS SALAD, TO FOIL YOUTH GROUP

CHURCH CLEANING

THINGS YOU MAY NEED

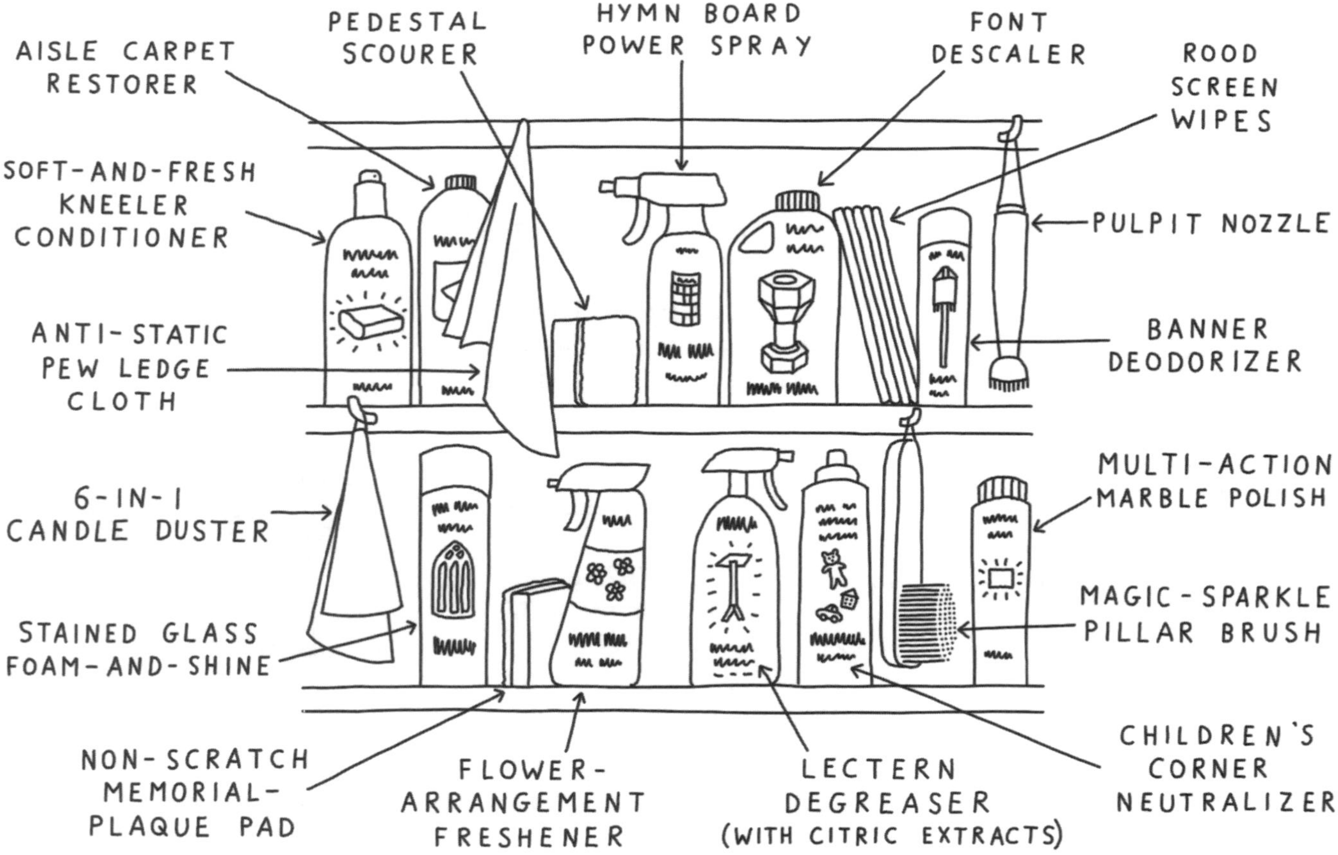
AISLE CARPET RESTORER
PEDESTAL SCOURER
HYMN BOARD POWER SPRAY
FONT DESCALER
ROOD SCREEN WIPES
SOFT-AND-FRESH KNEELER CONDITIONER
PULPIT NOZZLE
ANTI-STATIC PEW LEDGE CLOTH
BANNER DEODORIZER
6-IN-1 CANDLE DUSTER
MULTI-ACTION MARBLE POLISH
MAGIC-SPARKLE PILLAR BRUSH
STAINED GLASS FOAM-AND-SHINE
NON-SCRATCH MEMORIAL-PLAQUE PAD
FLOWER-ARRANGEMENT FRESHENER
LECTERN DEGREASER (WITH CITRIC EXTRACTS)
CHILDREN'S CORNER NEUTRALIZER

GROWING UP
IN A VICARAGE

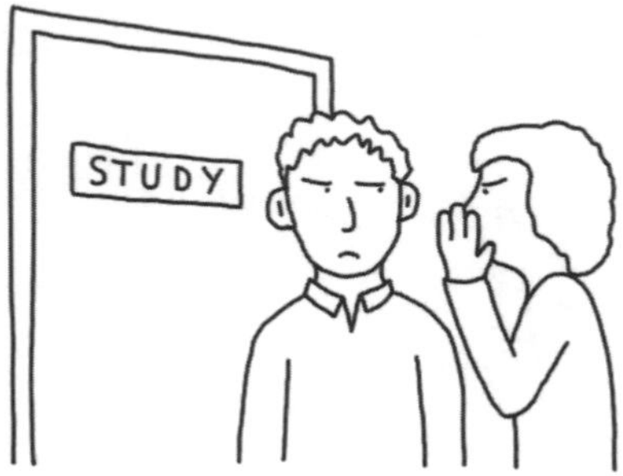
STUDY

WHISPERED ARGUMENTS, SO AS NOT TO DISTURB VERY IMPORTANT MEETINGS

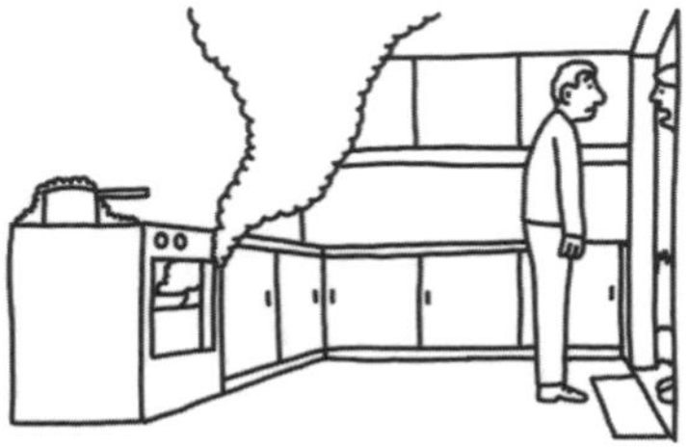

COOKING MISHAPS OWING TO UNEXPECTED PEOPLE AT THE DOOR

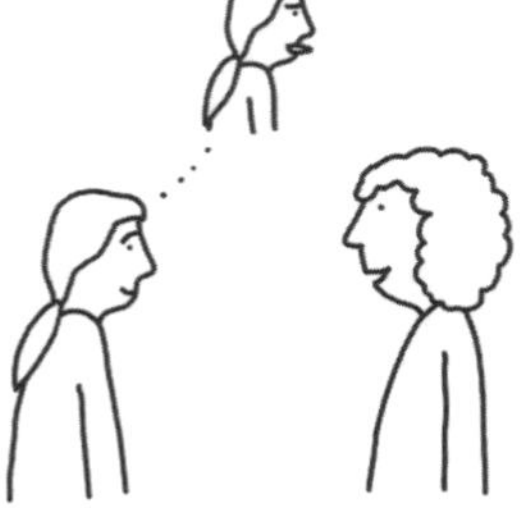

HAVING TO BE VERY POLITE

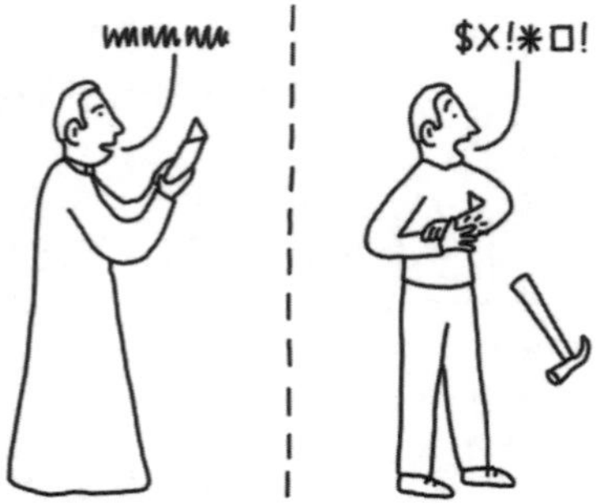
$X!✱□!

TRADITIONAL AND NON-TRADITIONAL LANGUAGE

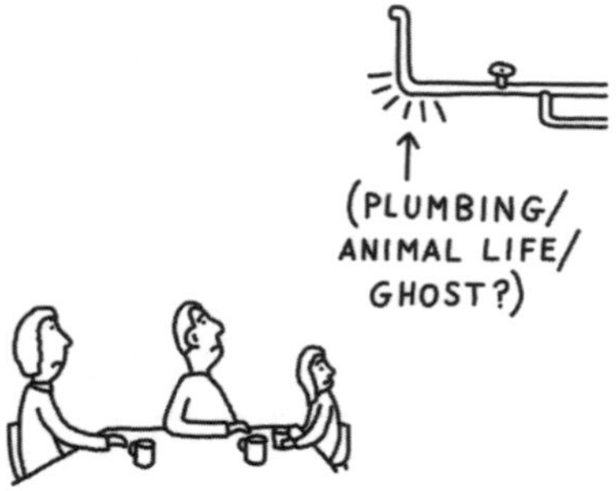
(PLUMBING/
ANIMAL LIFE/
GHOST?)

UNEXPLAINED NOISES

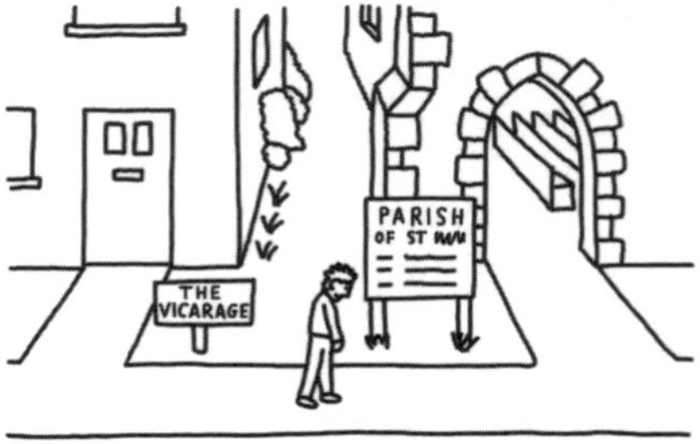
PARISH
OF ST
THE VICARAGE

BEING LATE FOR COMPULSORY CHURCH ATTENDANCE

VIRTUAL REALITY

PASSING THE
COLLECTION PLATE

ARRANGING THE FLOWERS

SHARING THE PEACE

PREACHING A SERMON

ARRIVING A BIT LATE

PERFORMING A
LITURGICAL DANCE

PHOTOGRAPHY

PERMITTED

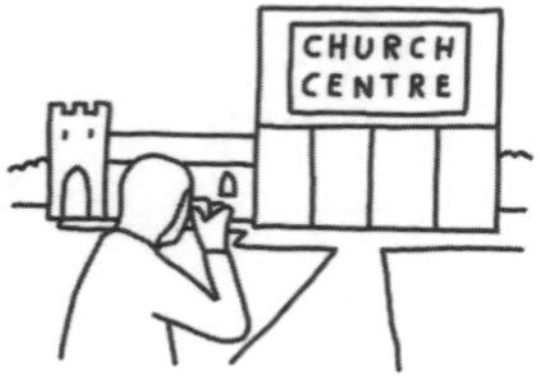
CHURCH
CENTRE

STUDIES OF THE ARCHITECTURE

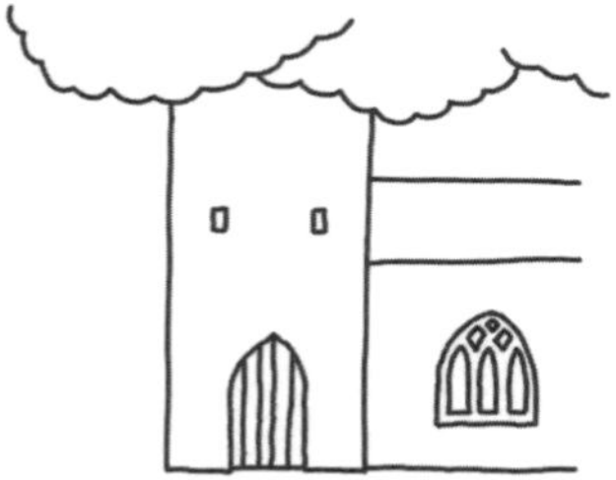

PANORAMAS FROM THE TOWER

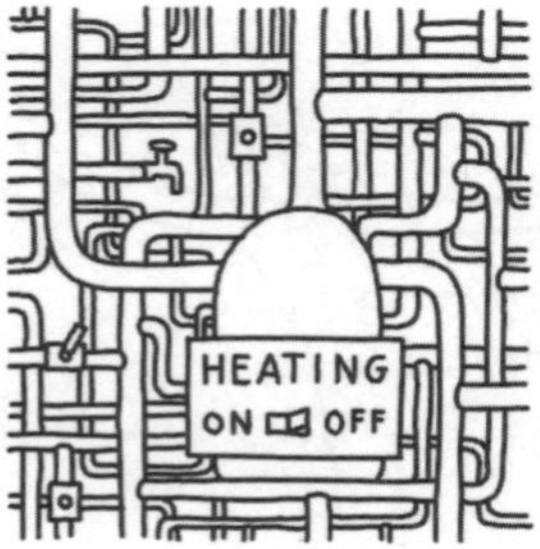
HEATING
ON OFF

SHOTS OF HISTORICAL ARTEFACTS

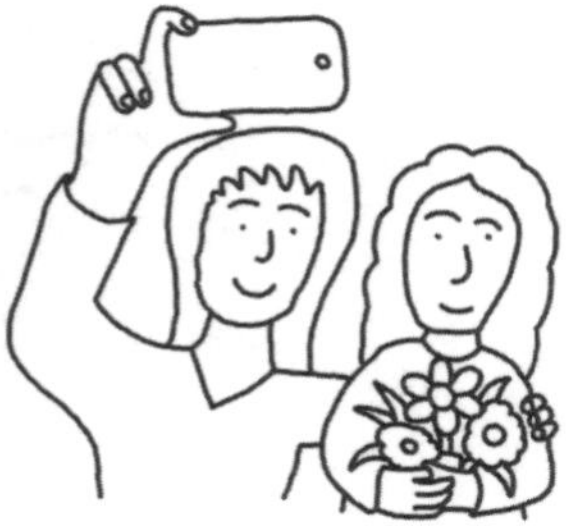

SELFIES WITH FLOWER ARRANGERS

NOT PERMITTED

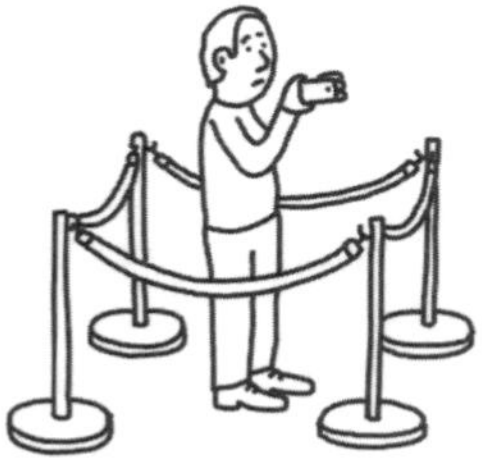

BREACHING THE BARRIERS

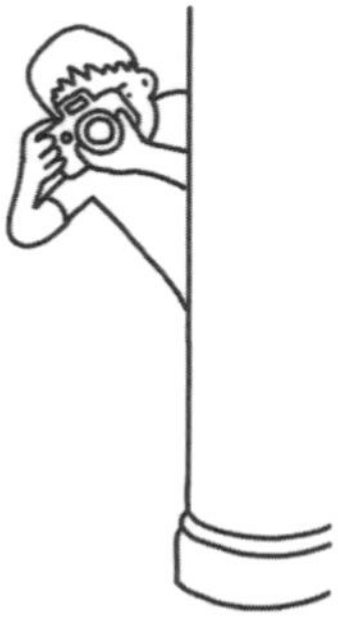

DISTRACTIONS DURING SERVICES

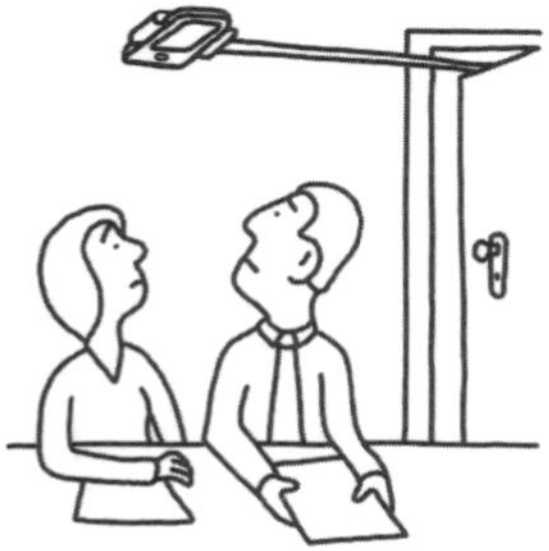

RECORDS OF CONFIDENTIAL MEETINGS

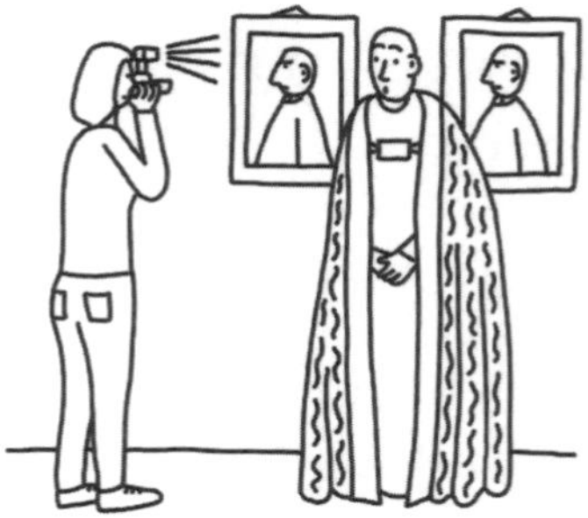

USING FLASH NEAR DELICATE ANTIQUITIES

THE NEIGHBOURING PARISHES

THINGS WE HAVE HEARD

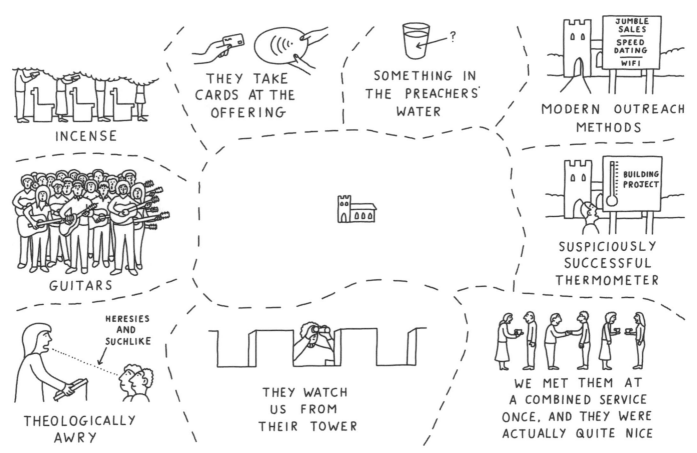

INCENSE

GUITARS

HERESIES AND SUCHLIKE

THEOLOGICALLY AWRY

THEY TAKE CARDS AT THE OFFERING

SOMETHING IN THE PREACHERS' WATER

THEY WATCH US FROM THEIR TOWER

JUMBLE SALES
SPEED DATING
WIFI

MODERN OUTREACH METHODS

BUILDING PROJECT

SUSPICIOUSLY SUCCESSFUL THERMOMETER

WE MET THEM AT A COMBINED SERVICE ONCE, AND THEY WERE ACTUALLY QUITE NICE

EVANGELICALS

HOW THEY ARE TAKING OVER

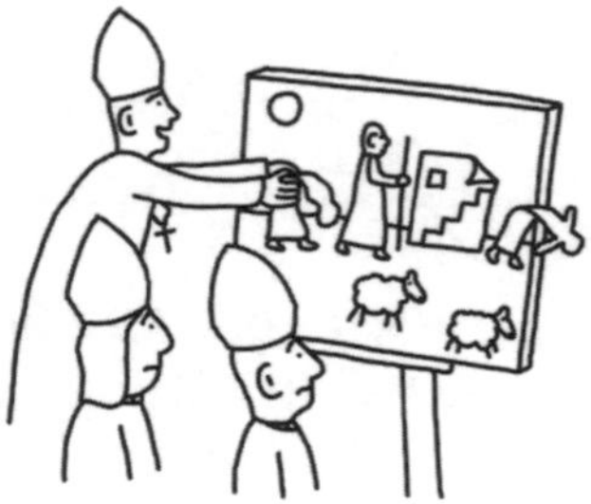

AN OUTBREAK OF FUZZY FELT AT THE BISHOPS' MEETING

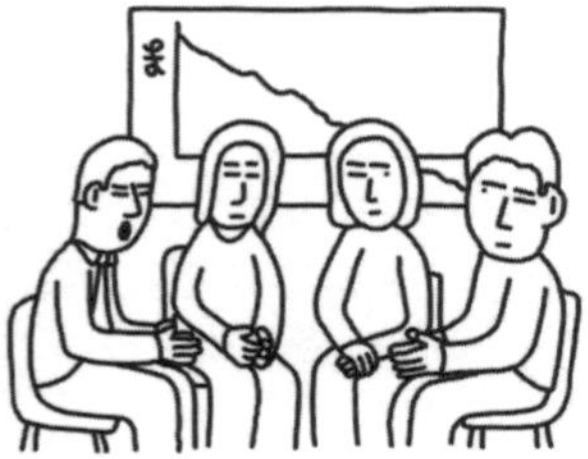

AN ERUPTION OF SPONTANEOUS OPEN PRAYER AT THE FINANCE COMMITTEE

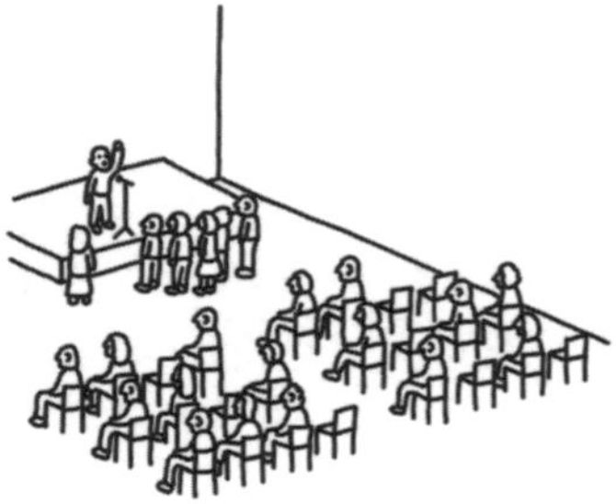

AN ALTAR CALL AT DEANERY SYNOD

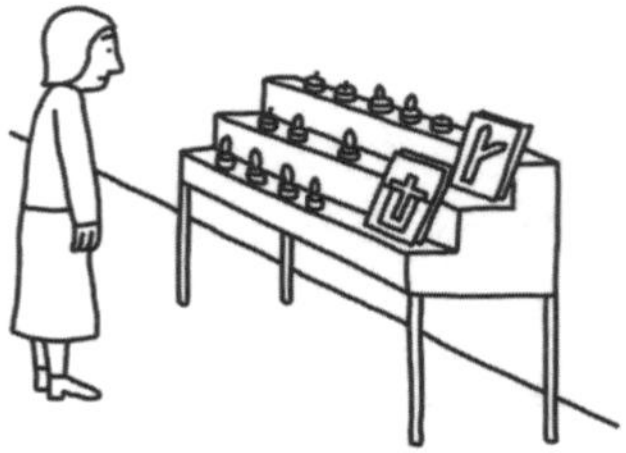

THE MYSTERIOUS APPEARANCE OF TRACTS IN THE CATHEDRAL

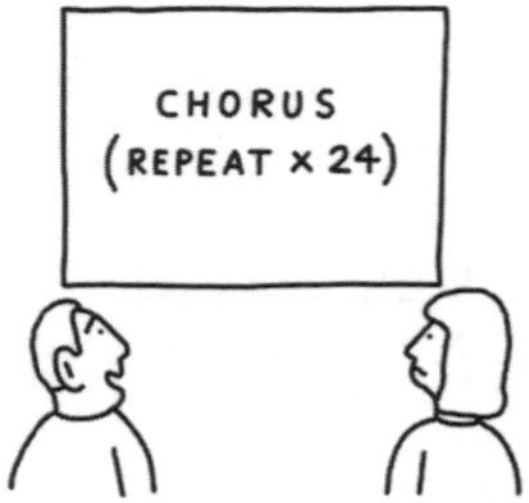

CHORUS
(REPEAT x 24)

WORSHIP INNOVATIONS AT THE CLERGY CONFERENCE

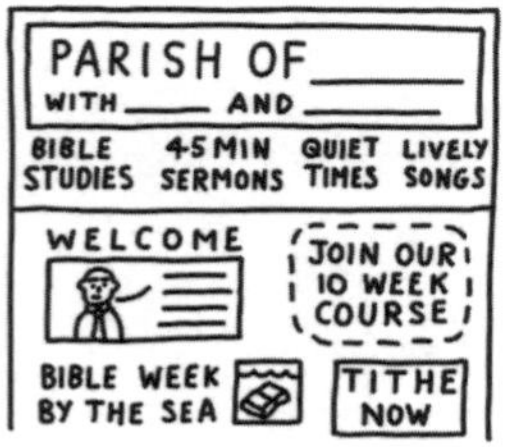

PARISH OF ______
WITH ____ AND ______
BIBLE STUDIES
45 MIN SERMONS
QUIET TIMES
LIVELY SONGS
WELCOME
JOIN OUR 10 WEEK COURSE
BIBLE WEEK BY THE SEA
TITHE NOW

SUBTLE CHANGES TO THE CHURCH WEBSITE TEMPLATE

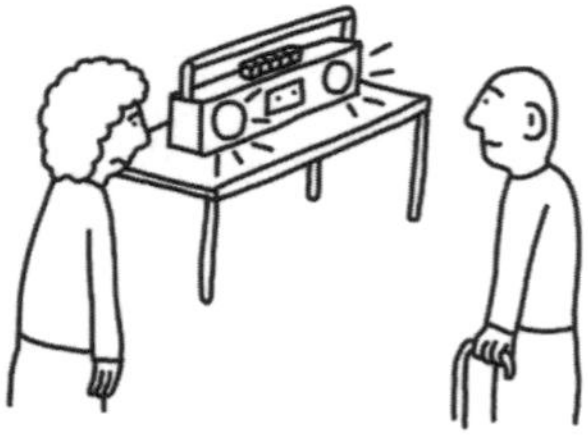

THE RELEASE OF A DIOCESAN EVANGELISTIC SINGLE

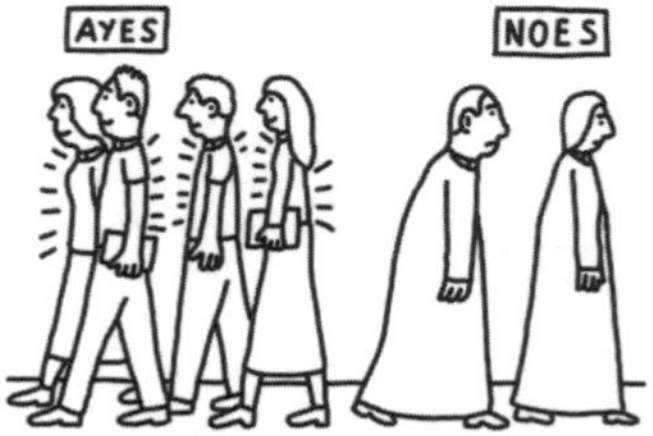

AYES
NOES

A GENERAL SYNOD MOTION FOR MANDATORY PASTEL CLERGY SHIRTS

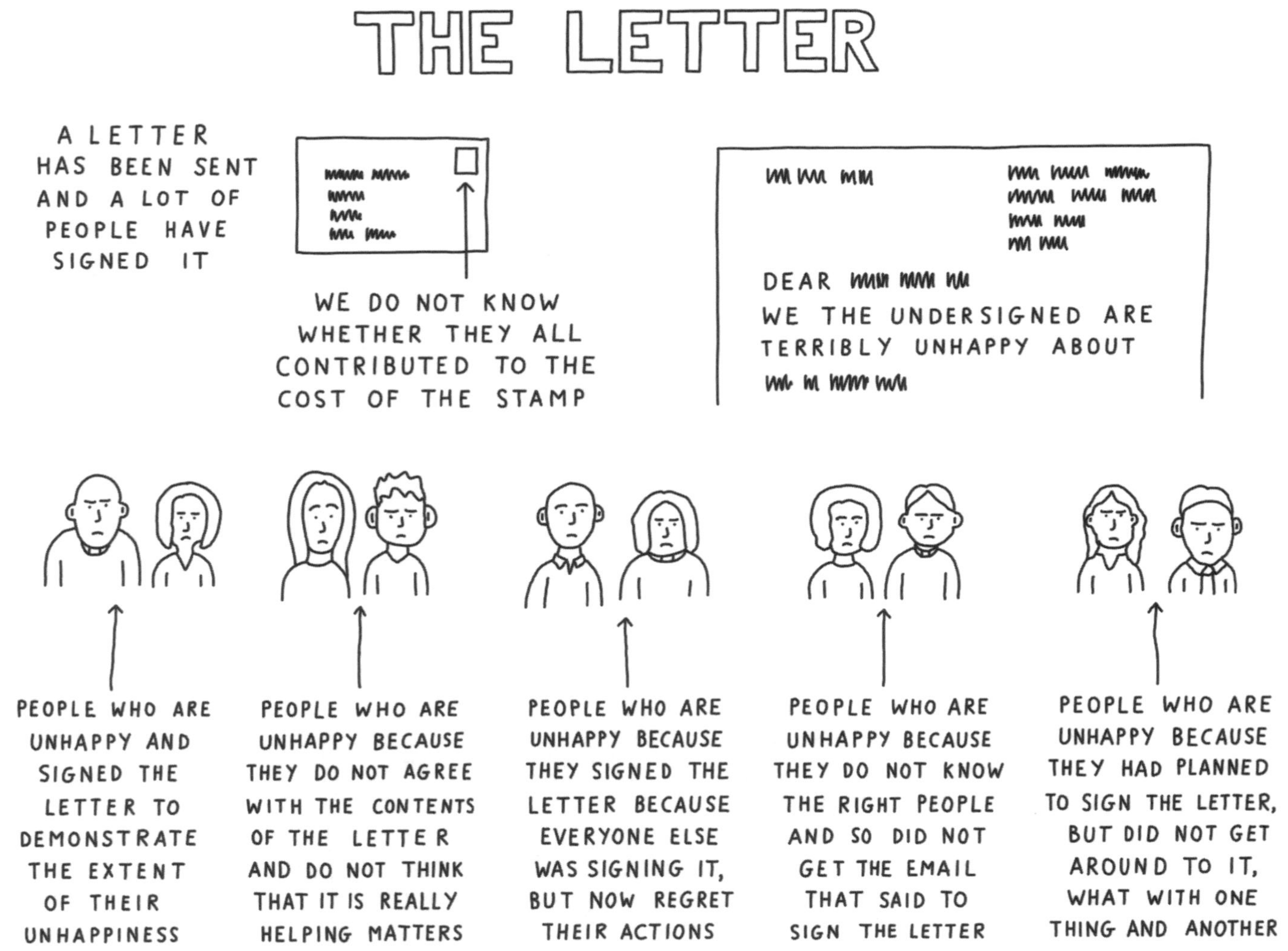
THE LETTER
A LETTER HAS BEEN SENT AND A LOT OF PEOPLE HAVE SIGNED IT
WE DO NOT KNOW WHETHER THEY ALL CONTRIBUTED TO THE COST OF THE STAMP
DEAR
WE THE UNDERSIGNED ARE TERRIBLY UNHAPPY ABOUT
PEOPLE WHO ARE UNHAPPY AND SIGNED THE LETTER TO DEMONSTRATE THE EXTENT OF THEIR UNHAPPINESS
PEOPLE WHO ARE UNHAPPY BECAUSE THEY DO NOT AGREE WITH THE CONTENTS OF THE LETTER AND DO NOT THINK THAT IT IS REALLY HELPING MATTERS
PEOPLE WHO ARE UNHAPPY BECAUSE THEY SIGNED THE LETTER BECAUSE EVERYONE ELSE WAS SIGNING IT, BUT NOW REGRET THEIR ACTIONS
PEOPLE WHO ARE UNHAPPY BECAUSE THEY DO NOT KNOW THE RIGHT PEOPLE AND SO DID NOT GET THE EMAIL THAT SAID TO SIGN THE LETTER
PEOPLE WHO ARE UNHAPPY BECAUSE THEY HAD PLANNED TO SIGN THE LETTER, BUT DID NOT GET AROUND TO IT, WHAT WITH ONE THING AND ANOTHER

THE FOODBANK

WAYS YOU CAN HELP

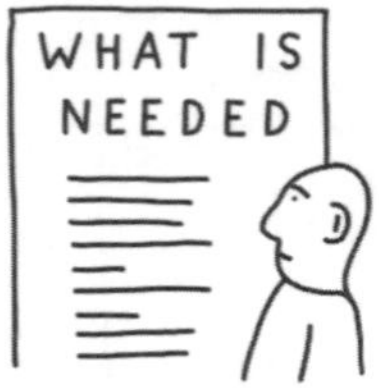
WHAT IS NEEDED

FIND OUT WHAT IS NEEDED

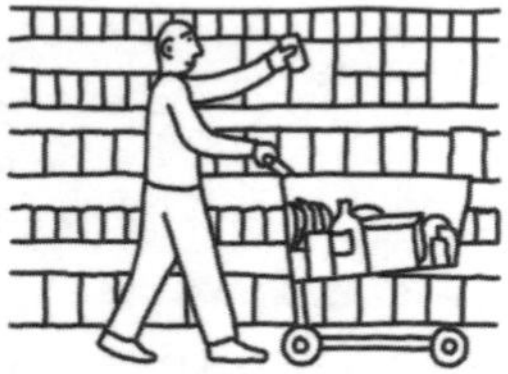

PICK UP EXTRA ITEMS WHEN YOU SHOP

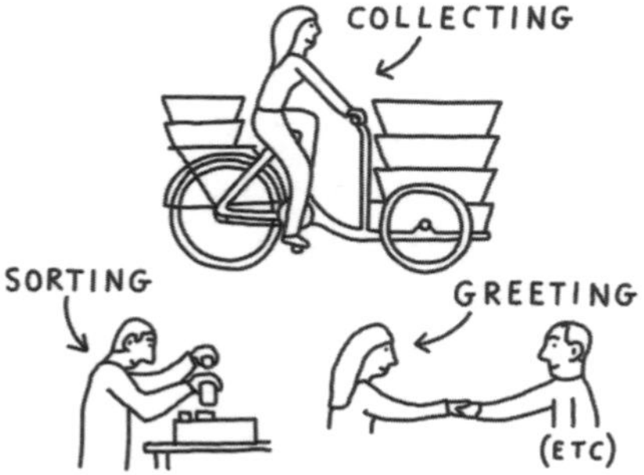
COLLECTING
SORTING
GREETING
(ETC)

VOLUNTEER

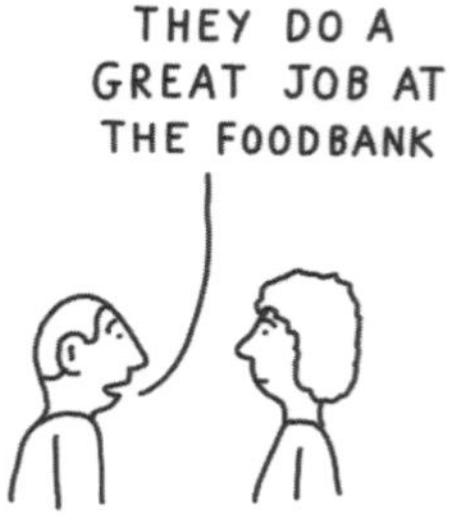
THEY DO A GREAT JOB AT THE FOODBANK

GOSSIP POSITIVELY

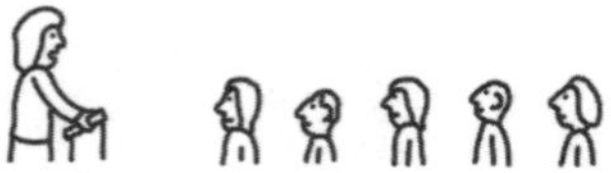

INVITE SOMEONE FROM THE FOODBANK TO TALK TO YOUR CHURCH OR GROUP

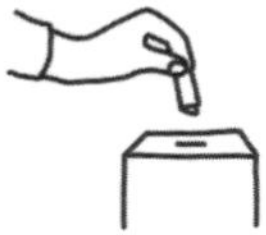

DONATE MONEY

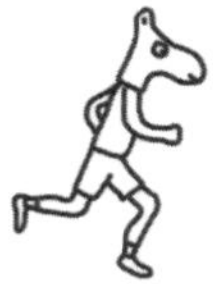

FUNDRAISE

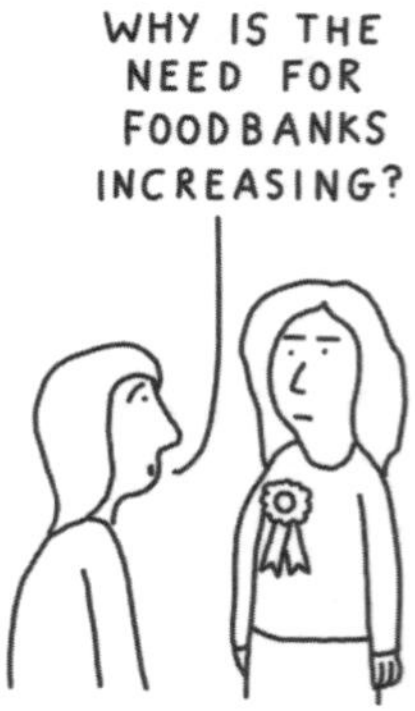
WHY IS THE NEED FOR FOODBANKS INCREASING?

ASK AWKWARD QUESTIONS

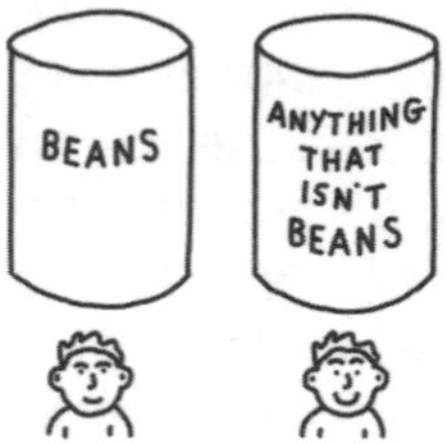
BEANS
ANYTHING THAT ISN'T BEANS

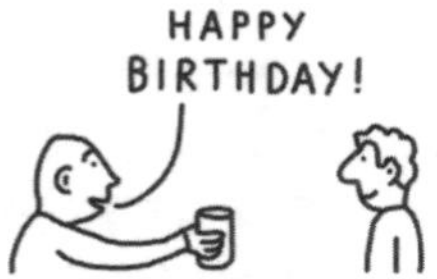
HAPPY BIRTHDAY!

ASK PEOPLE FOR FOODBANK DONATIONS RATHER THAN PRESENTS

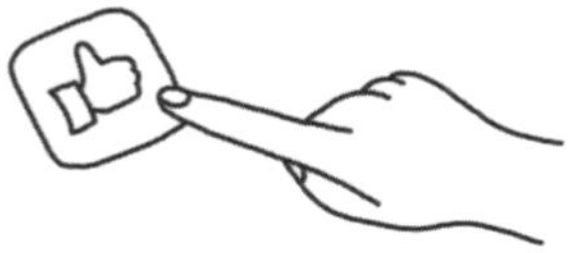

LIKE THE SOCIAL MEDIA PAGE

BREXIT

ECCLESIASTICAL METAPHORS

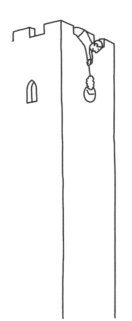

DANGER OF
FALLING FROM
A GREAT HEIGHT
WHILST
CONDUCTING
UNNECESSARY
TASK

MINISTER
ENCOURAGING
BELIEF

NO
SERMON   NO
COFFEE   NO
SUNDAY
SCHOOL
LEADERS   NO
← IDEA

ROTAS

GENERAL UNPREPAREDNESS

PRAYING
THAT
SOMEHOW
IT ALL
TURNS OUT
OK

LEAP OF
FAITH

HEADS BOWED
IN DESPAIR

CHURCH HOUSE

WHY IT IS A GOOD PLACE FOR A WARFARE CONFERENCE SPONSORED BY ARMS COMPANIES

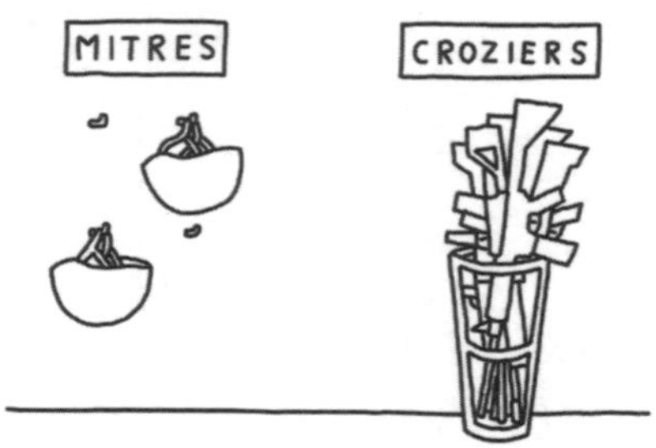
MITRES
CROZIERS

WELL-EQUIPPED AND ADAPTABLE BUILDING

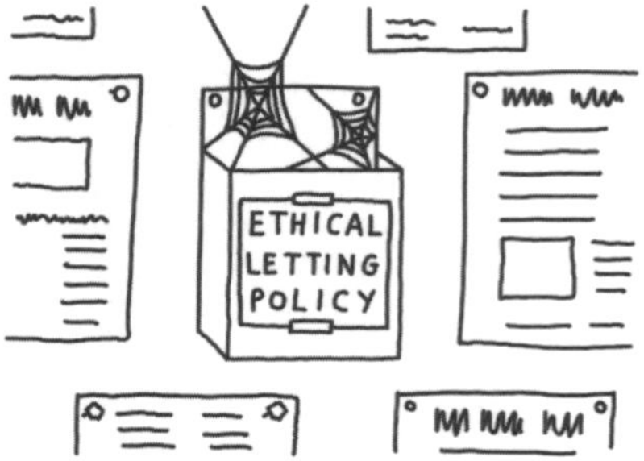
ETHICAL LETTING POLICY

REMARKABLY LITTLE RED TAPE

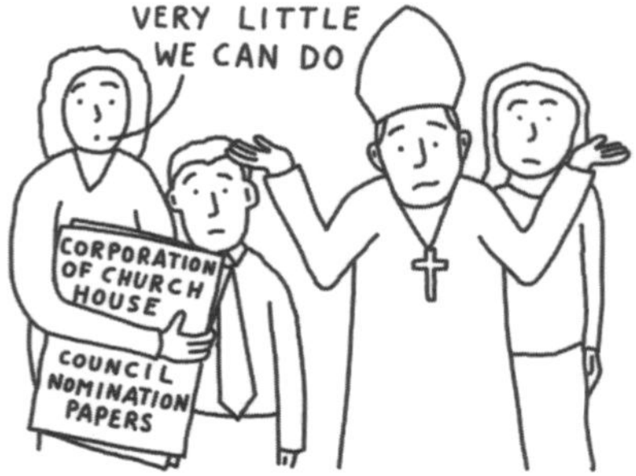
VERY LITTLE WE CAN DO
CORPORATION OF CHURCH HOUSE
COUNCIL NOMINATION PAPERS

DENIABILITY BY THE ARCHBISHOPS' COUNCIL

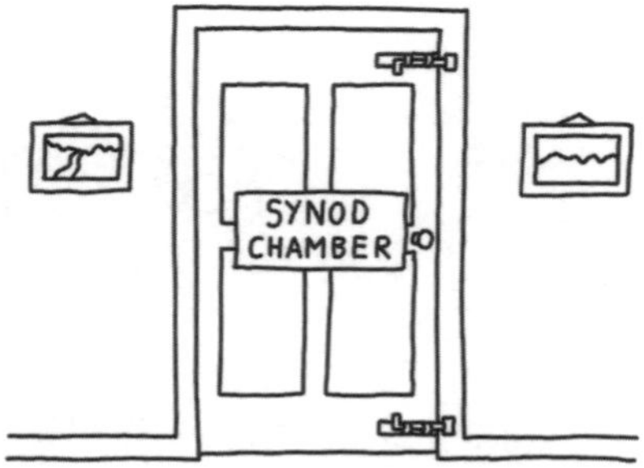
SYNOD CHAMBER

SPACE TO PUT PROTESTERS WHERE NO ONE IS LISTENING

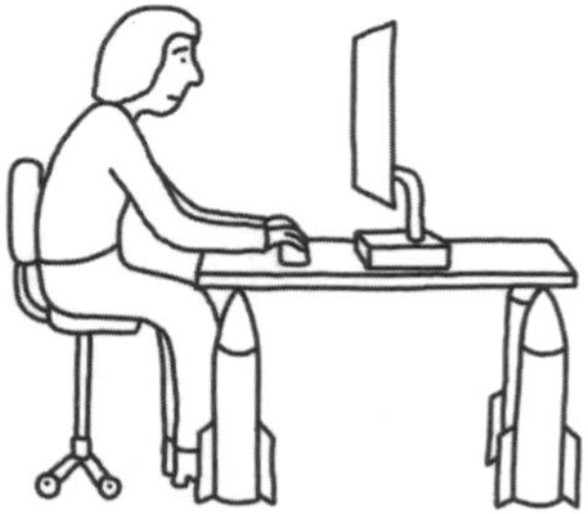

HELPS FUND OFFICE SPACE FOR THE C OF E

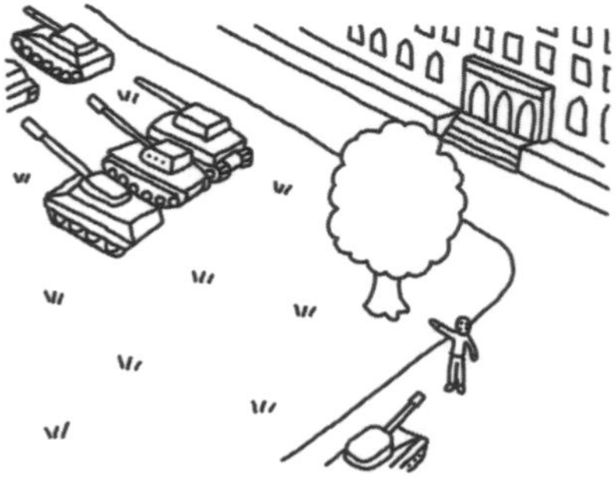

PLENTY OF ROOM FOR PARKING

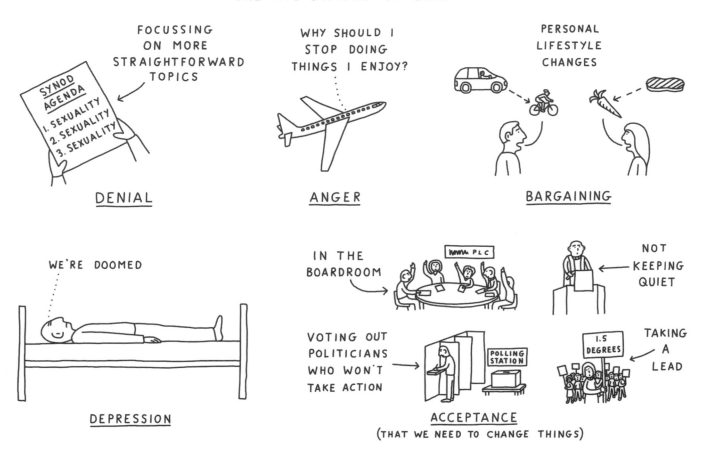

CLIMATE
THE FIVE STAGES OF GRIEF

FOCUSSING ON MORE STRAIGHTFORWARD TOPICS

SYNOD AGENDA
1. SEXUALITY
2. SEXUALITY
3. SEXUALITY

DENIAL

WHY SHOULD I STOP DOING THINGS I ENJOY?

ANGER

PERSONAL LIFESTYLE CHANGES

BARGAINING

WE'RE DOOMED

DEPRESSION

IN THE BOARDROOM

PLC

NOT KEEPING QUIET

VOTING OUT POLITICIANS WHO WON'T TAKE ACTION

POLLING STATION

1.5 DEGREES

TAKING A LEAD

ACCEPTANCE
(THAT WE NEED TO CHANGE THINGS)

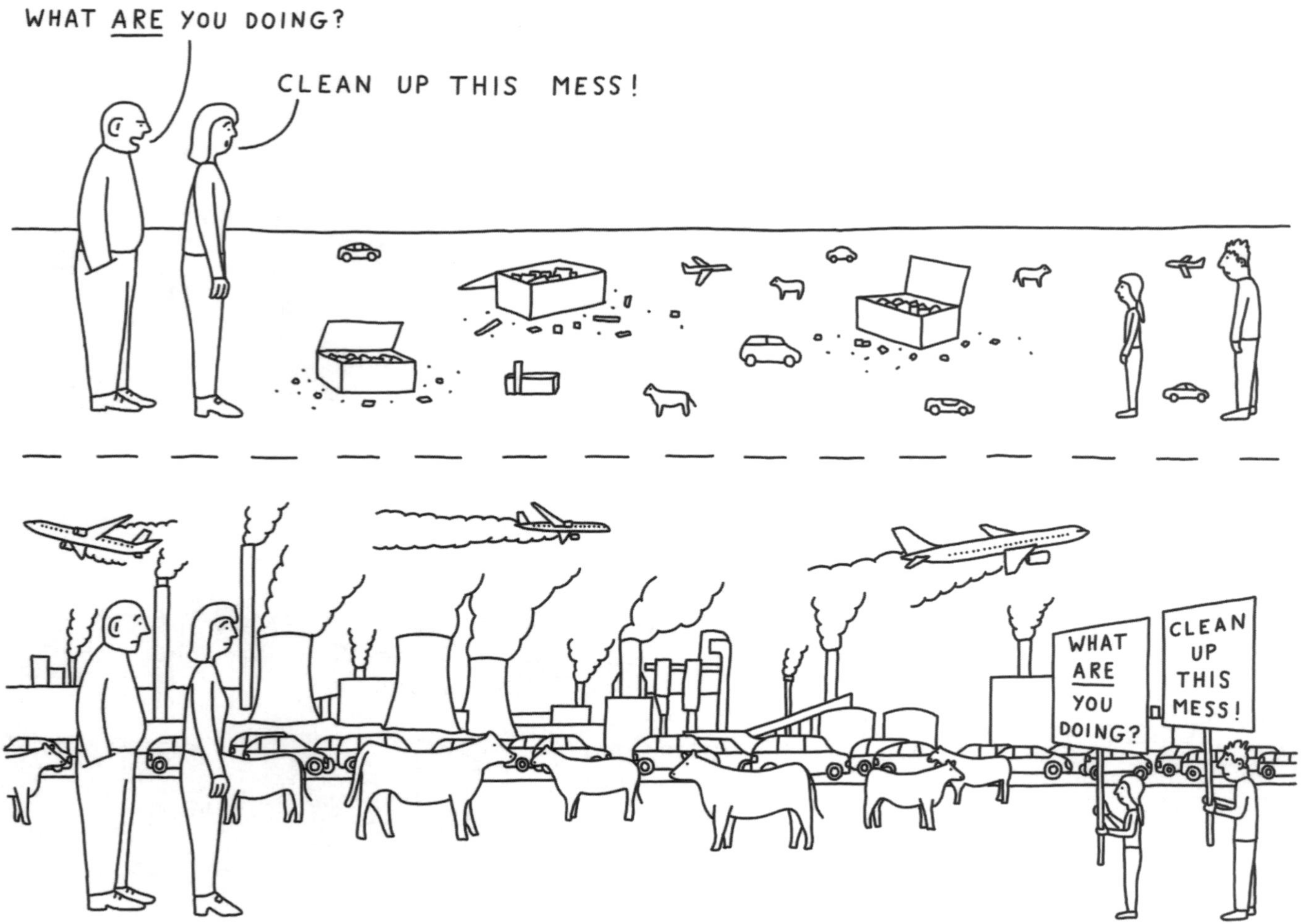
WHAT ARE YOU DOING?
CLEAN UP THIS MESS!
WHAT ARE YOU DOING?
CLEAN UP THIS MESS!

GO IN PEACE...

10.45 AM

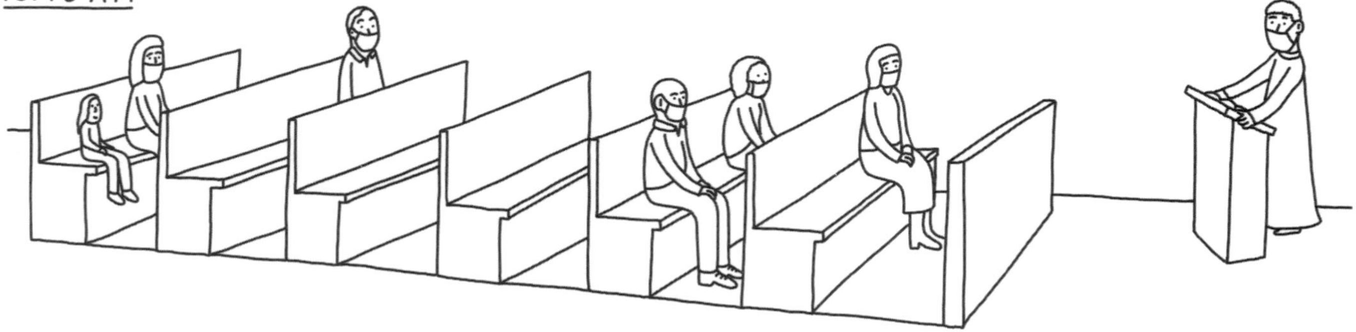

10.55 AM

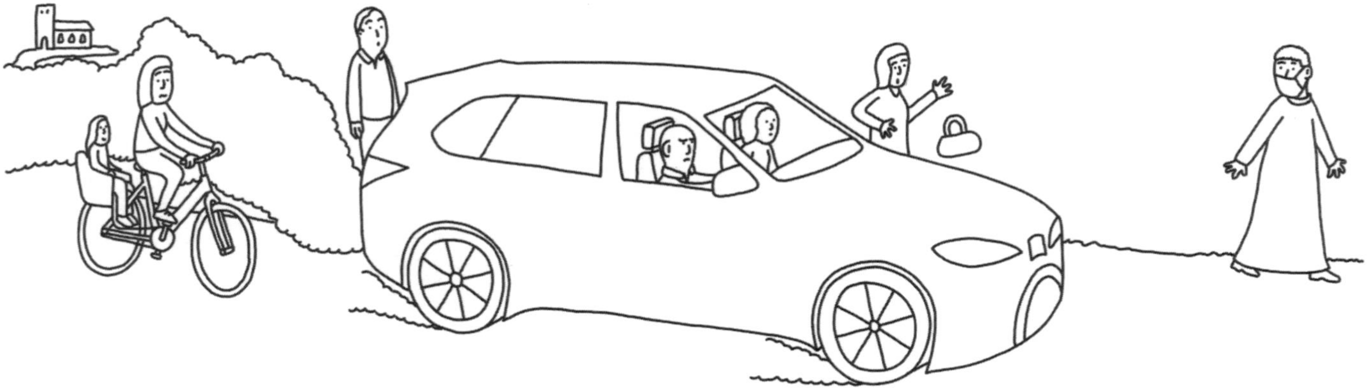

PART TWO: THE PANDEMIC

CHURCH SERVICES

WAYS TO HOLD THEM DURING A PANDEMIC

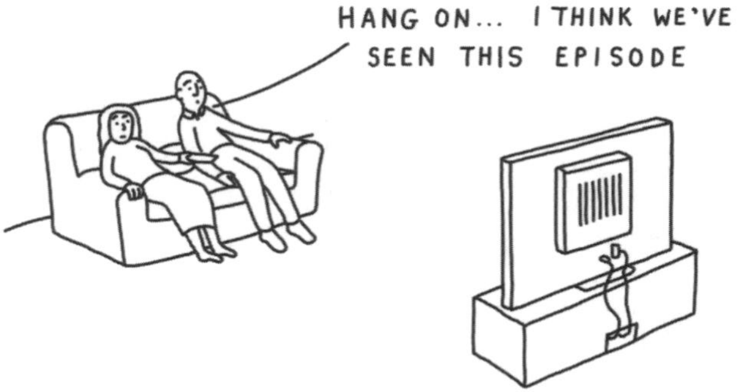
HANG ON... I THINK WE'VE SEEN THIS EPISODE

ONLINE (RECORDED)

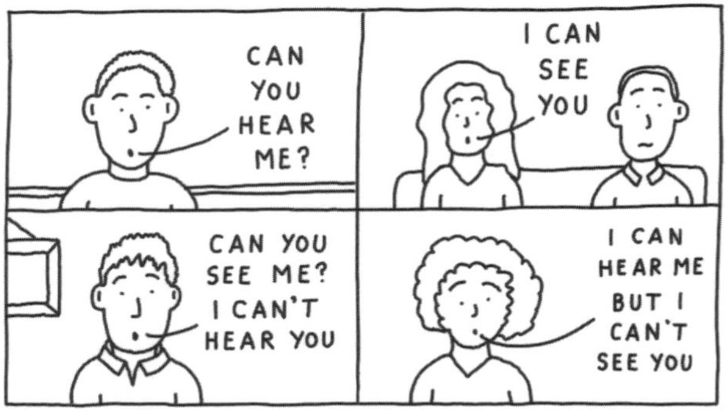
CAN YOU HEAR ME?
I CAN SEE YOU
CAN YOU SEE ME? I CAN'T HEAR YOU
I CAN HEAR ME BUT I CAN'T SEE YOU

ONLINE (LIVE)

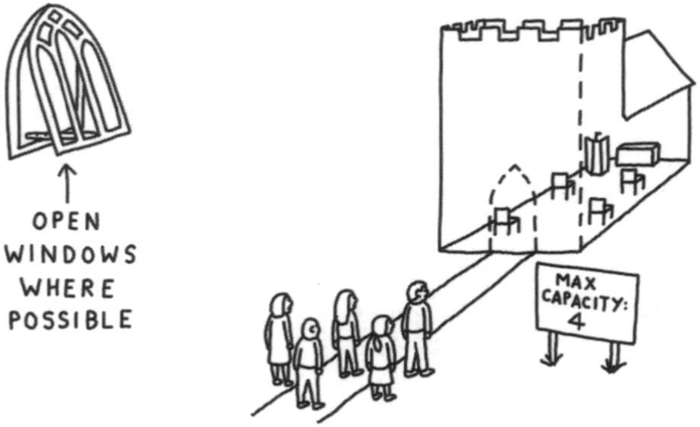
OPEN WINDOWS WHERE POSSIBLE
MAX CAPACITY: 4

IN THE BUILDING

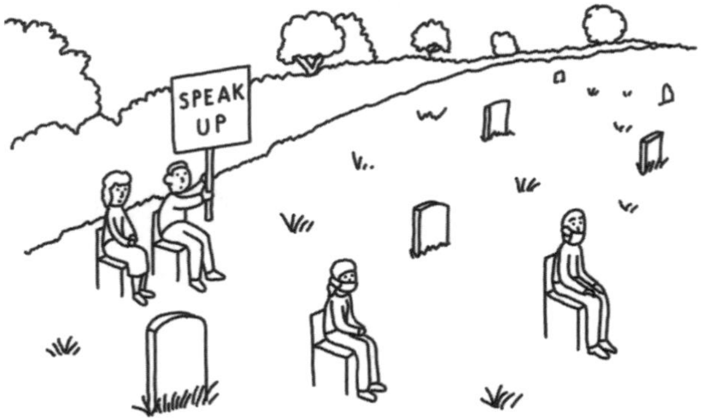
SPEAK UP

OUTDOORS

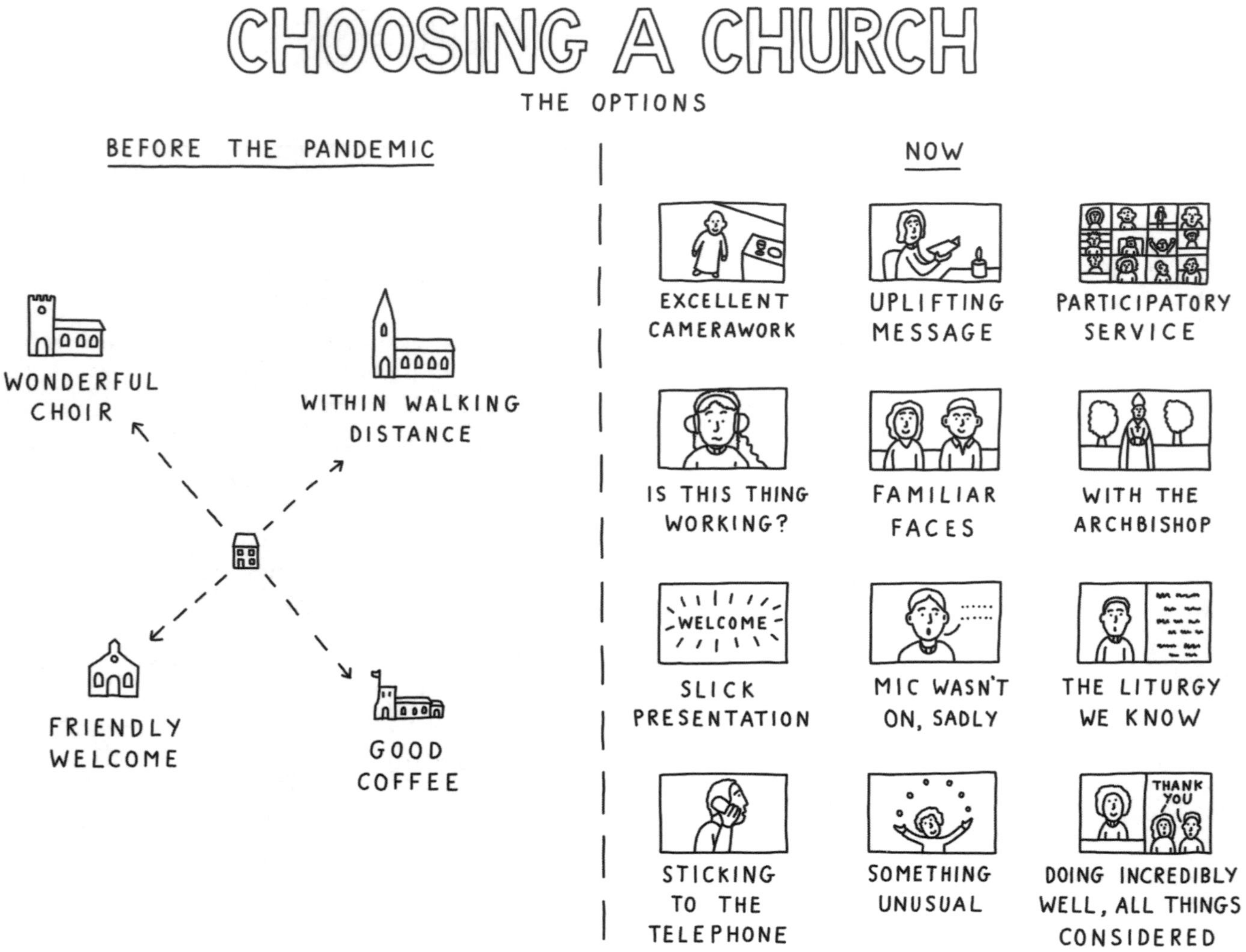
CHOOSING A CHURCH
THE OPTIONS
BEFORE THE PANDEMIC
WONDERFUL CHOIR
WITHIN WALKING DISTANCE
FRIENDLY WELCOME
GOOD COFFEE
NOW
EXCELLENT CAMERAWORK
UPLIFTING MESSAGE
PARTICIPATORY SERVICE
IS THIS THING WORKING?
FAMILIAR FACES
WITH THE ARCHBISHOP
WELCOME
SLICK PRESENTATION
MIC WASN'T ON, SADLY
THE LITURGY WE KNOW
STICKING TO THE TELEPHONE
SOMETHING UNUSUAL
THANK YOU
DOING INCREDIBLY WELL, ALL THINGS CONSIDERED

ONLINE SERVICES

THINGS THAT CAN GO TERRIBLY WRONG

PROBLEMS WITH THE SOUND

CONFIDENTIAL
ACCIDENTAL SCREEN-SHARING OF PASTORALLY-SENSITIVE INFORMATION

THE MAIN THING I WANT TO SAY IS...
NOT FOUND
INTERNET BREAKS AT CRUCIAL MOMENT

LET US PRAY...
LINDA! HAVE YOU SEEN MY SPECTACLES?
FAILING TO MUTE THE CONGREGATION

WELCOME TO THE
ANIMALS RUNNING AMOK

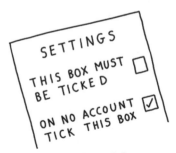

SETTINGS
THIS BOX MUST BE TICKED
ON NO ACCOUNT TICK THIS BOX
THE APP HASN'T BEEN CONFIGURED

THAT'S ONE WORSHIP VIDEO TOO MANY, SON
LIVE ARREST OWING TO IGNORING COPYRIGHT

INVASION BY ROWDY GROUP OF METHODISTS

CLERGY

WHAT THEY ARE DOING

PREACHING
MINISTRY

COORDINATING
FOOD PARCELS

TAKING A
BREAK

LOOKING AFTER
THE KIDS

CONDUCTING
NUMEROUS
MEETINGS

TELEPHONING
EVERYONE IN
THE PARISH

PRAYING/
WALKING AROUND
THE GARDEN

DOING THE BEST YOU
CAN, WHATEVER THAT
MIGHT INVOLVE

GOOD

ALSO GOOD

ROTAS

HOW TO RECREATE THEM AT HOME DURING LOCKDOWN

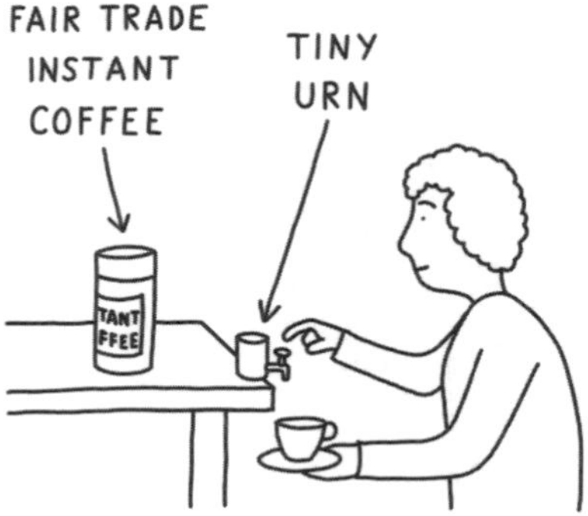
FAIR TRADE INSTANT COFFEE
TINY URN

COFFEE

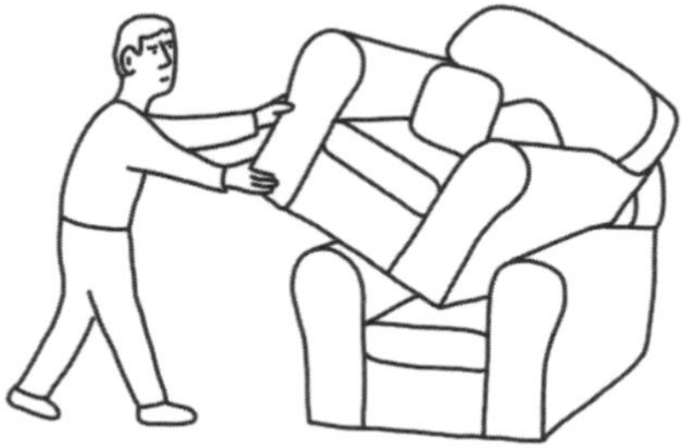

STACKING THE CHAIRS

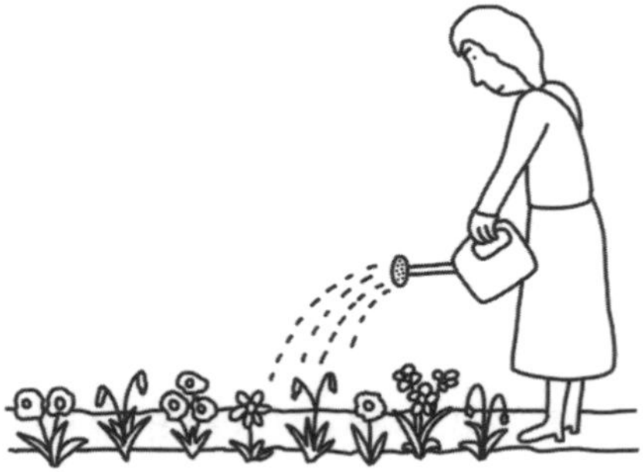

DOING THE FLOWERS

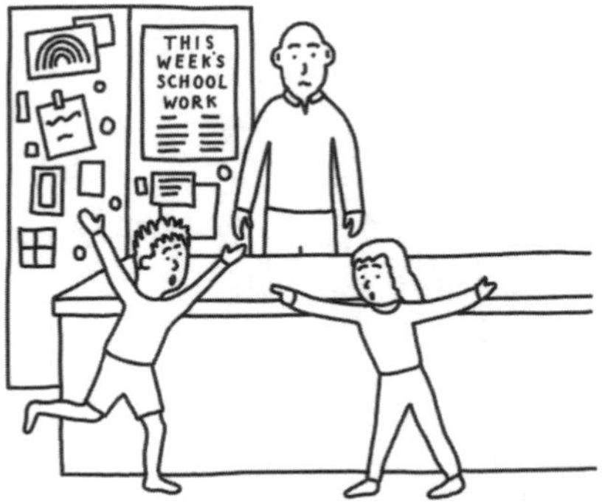
THIS WEEK'S SCHOOL WORK

SUNDAY SCHOOL

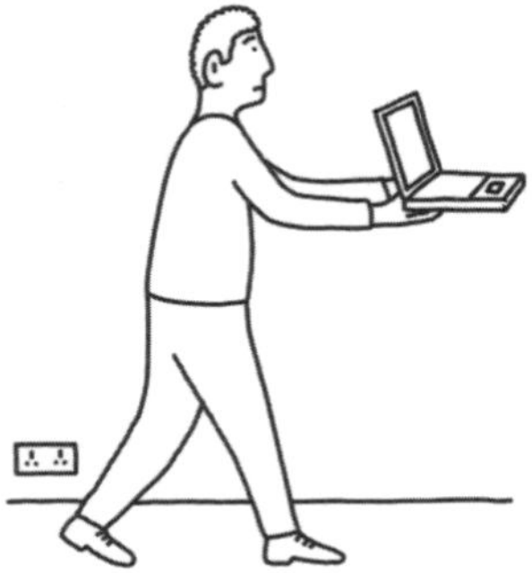

LITURGICAL DUTIES

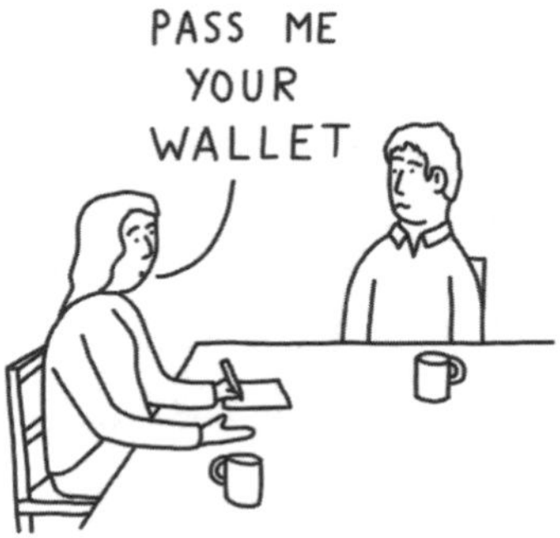
PASS ME YOUR WALLET

COUNTING THE COLLECTION

REMINDERS

OF FORGOTTEN CONCEPTS

THE HYMN BOOK

ALL OUR FAVOURITE THINGS TO SING
IN ONE VOLUME

THE PEW

SEAT FOR MORE THAN ONE PERSON,
NOT ALL FROM THE SAME HOUSEHOLD

THE PROCESSION

A FORMAL KIND OF WALKING, WITH
PARTICIPANTS OFTEN PAYING SCANT
ATTENTION TO SOCIAL-DISTANCING RULES

THE PEACE

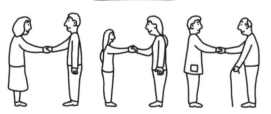

A TIME DURING A CHURCH SERVICE
WHEN EVERYONE STOPS AND SHAKES
HANDS FOR THE SHEER JOY OF IT

BACKGROUNDS

FOR BROADCASTING FROM THE CLERGY STUDY

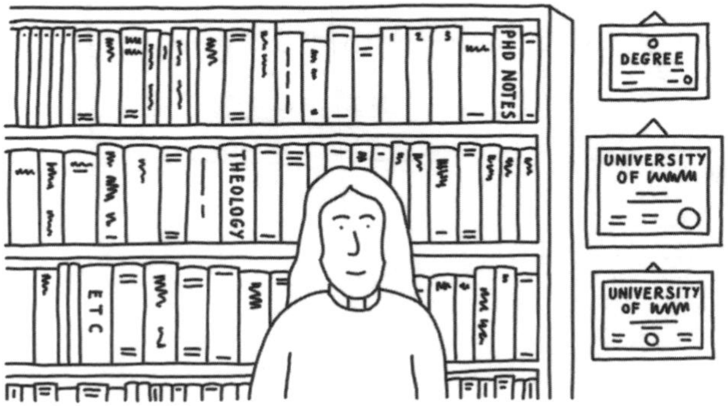
PHD NOTES
THEOLOGY
ETC
DEGREE
UNIVERSITY OF
UNIVERSITY OF

SCHOLARLY

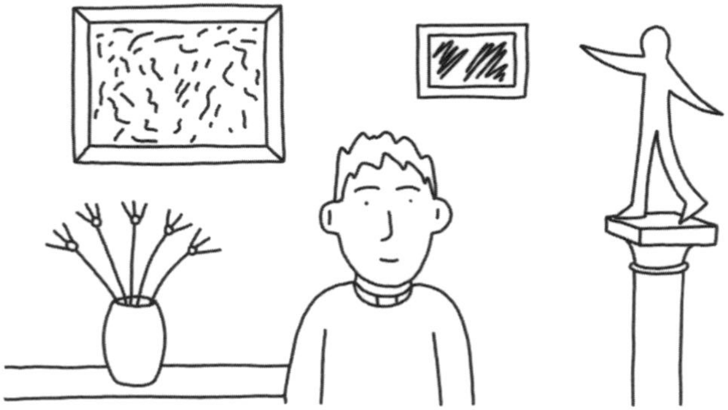

ARTISTIC

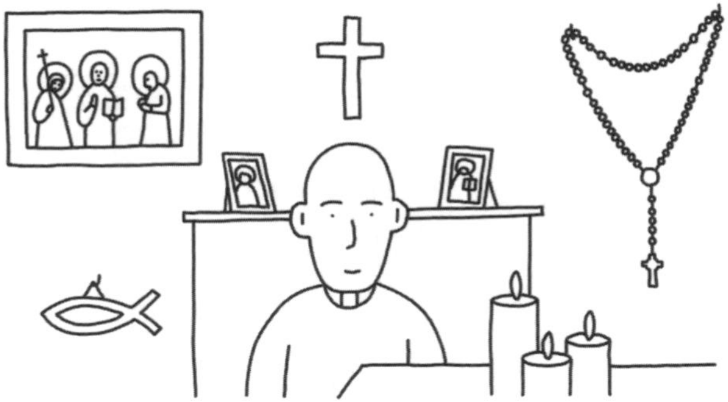

SPIRITUAL

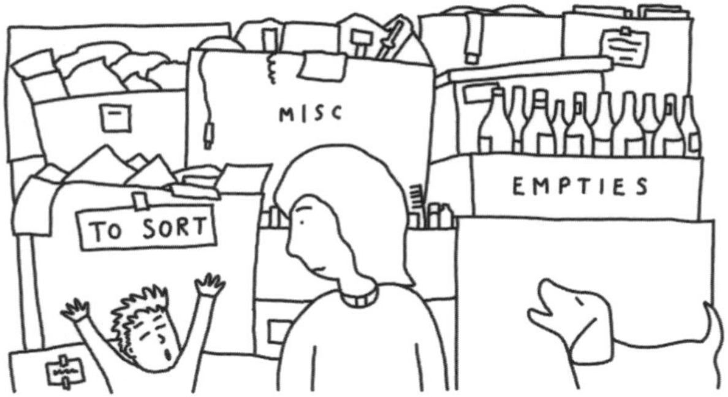
MISC
TO SORT
EMPTIES

REALISTIC

LIVESTREAMING THE SERVICE

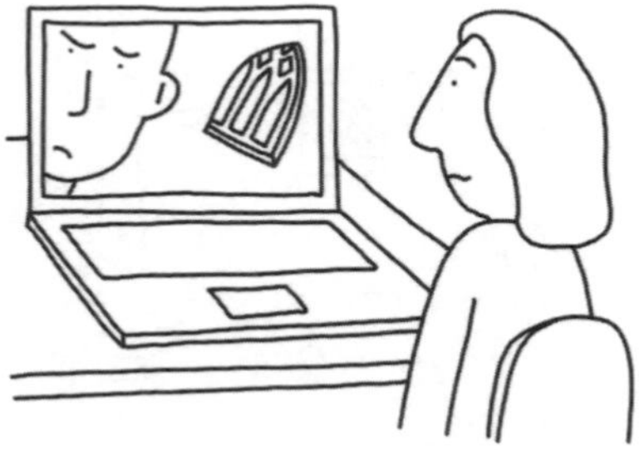

THE DIRECTOR'S CUT

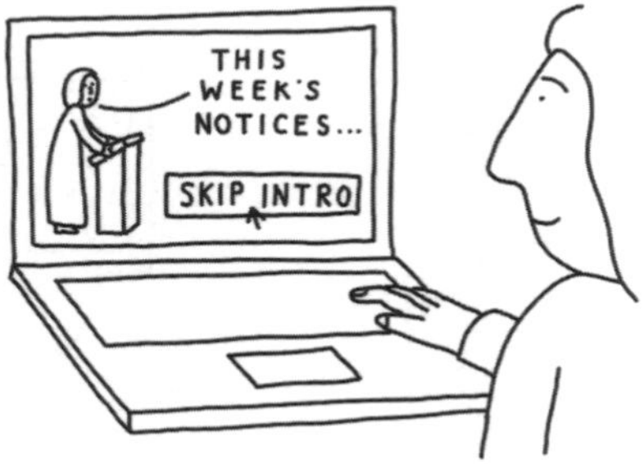
THIS WEEK'S NOTICES...
SKIP INTRO

OPENING CREDITS

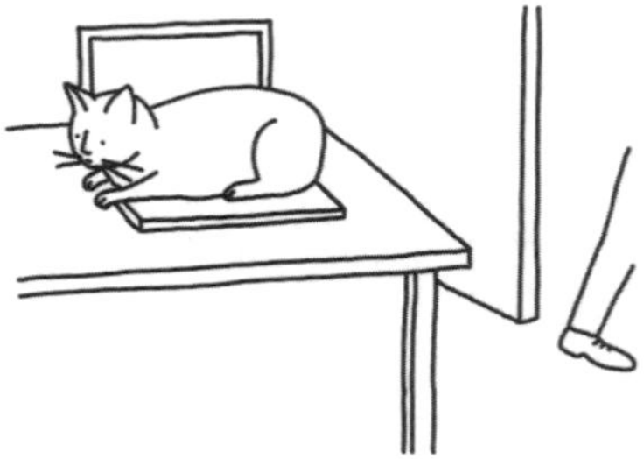

INTERVAL

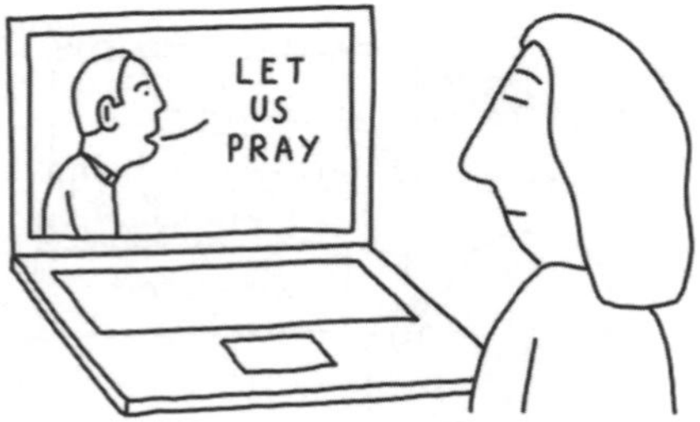
LET US PRAY

A BIT OF SHUT-EYE

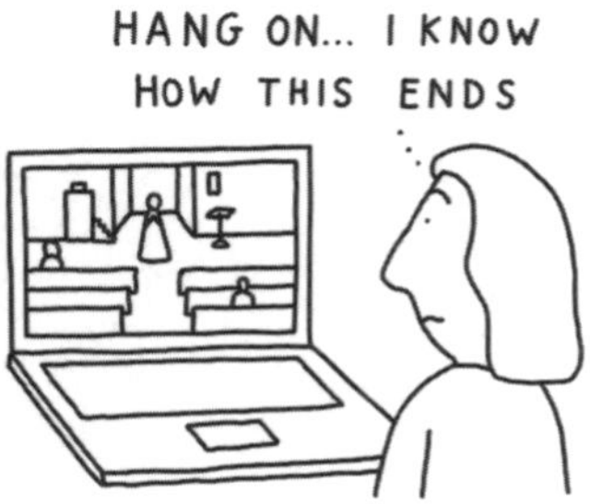
HANG ON... I KNOW HOW THIS ENDS

THE REALISATION THAT THIS WAS LAST WEEK'S EPISODE

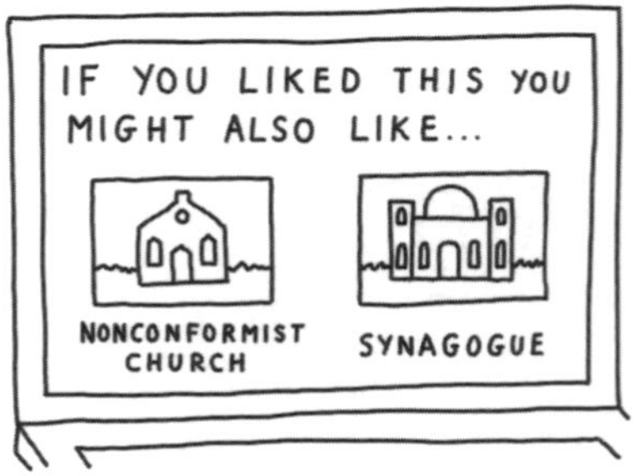
IF YOU LIKED THIS YOU MIGHT ALSO LIKE...
NONCONFORMIST CHURCH
SYNAGOGUE

RECOMMENDATIONS FOR FUTURE VIEWING

THE ONLINE SERVICE
HOW TO MAKE IT FEEL LIKE NORMAL

ARRIVE A FEW MINUTES
LATE, CARRYING COFFEE

SCOWL AT THE PERSON
SITTING IN YOUR SEAT

WHISPERED DISCIPLINING OF
CHILDREN (UNSUCCESSFUL)

USE YOUR PHONE TO
'READ THE BIBLE'

STAND UP AT ENTIRELY
THE WRONG POINT

SHARE A PLATE OF
STALE BISCUITS

THE CHURCH MEETING

COMMUNICATION LESSONS FROM GOVERNMENT BRIEFINGS

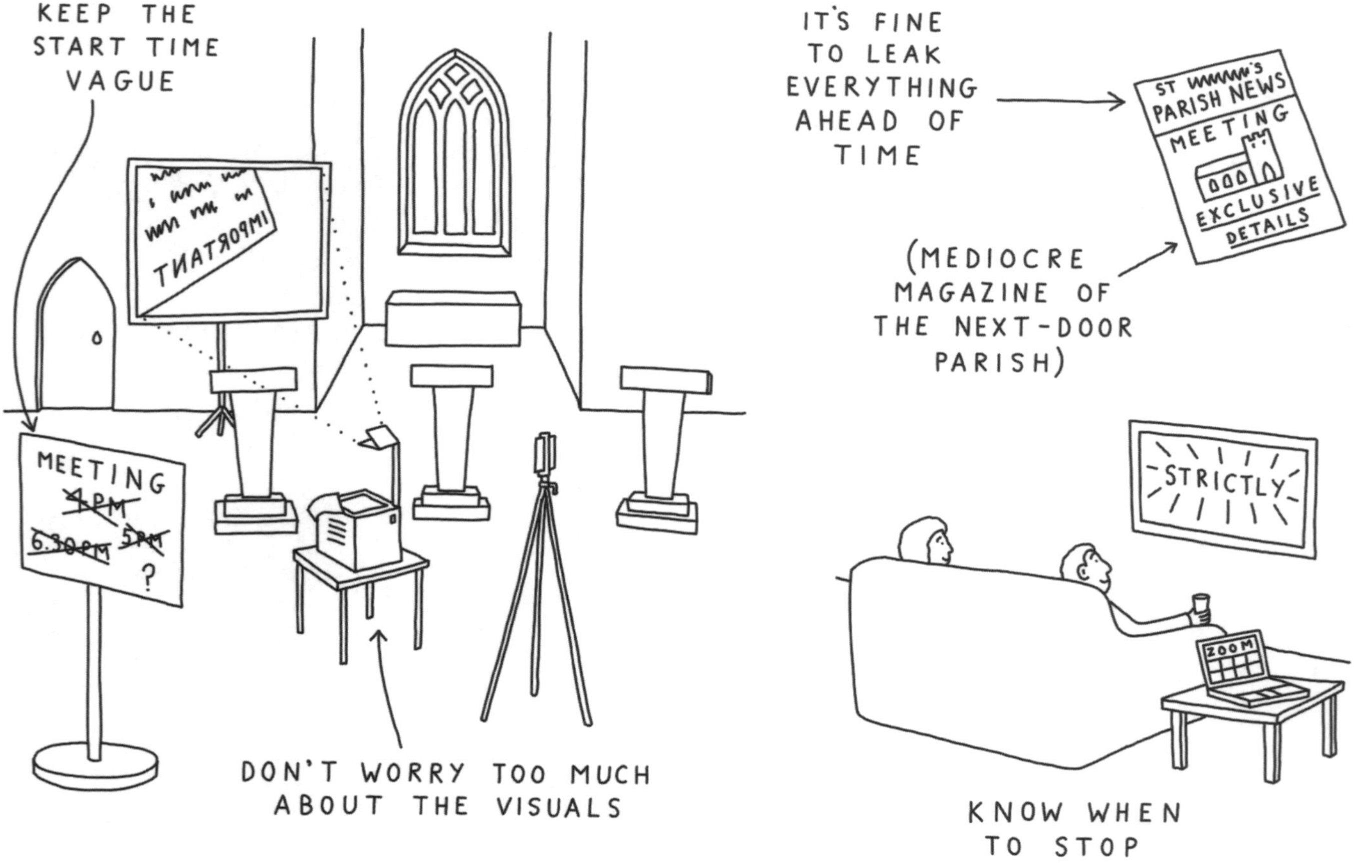
KEEP THE START TIME VAGUE
MEETING
?
IMPORTANT
DON'T WORRY TOO MUCH ABOUT THE VISUALS
IT'S FINE TO LEAK EVERYTHING AHEAD OF TIME
ST ...'S PARISH NEWS
MEETING
EXCLUSIVE DETAILS
(MEDIOCRE MAGAZINE OF THE NEXT-DOOR PARISH)
STRICTLY
ZOOM
KNOW WHEN TO STOP

THE ONLINE MEETING

APPEARANCE

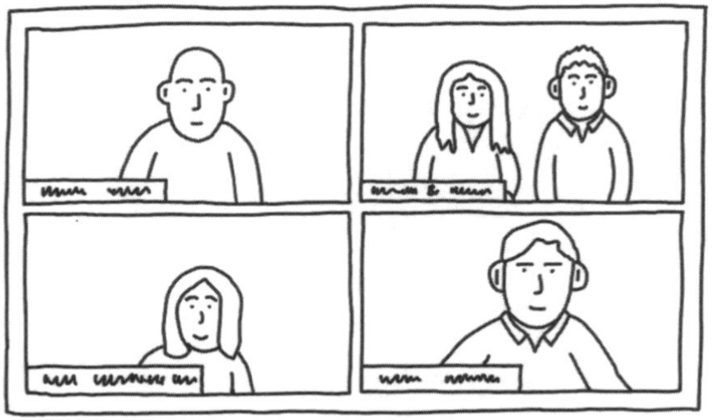

REALITY

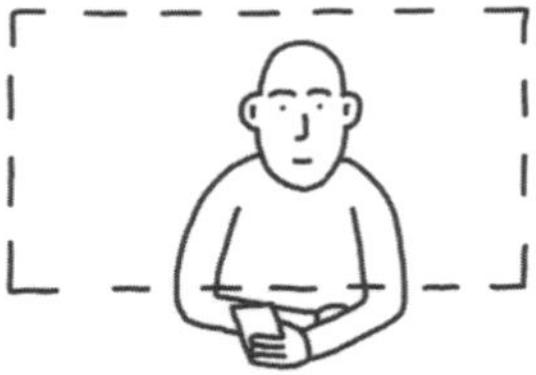

FOLLOWING TWITTER AND/OR THE FOOTBALL

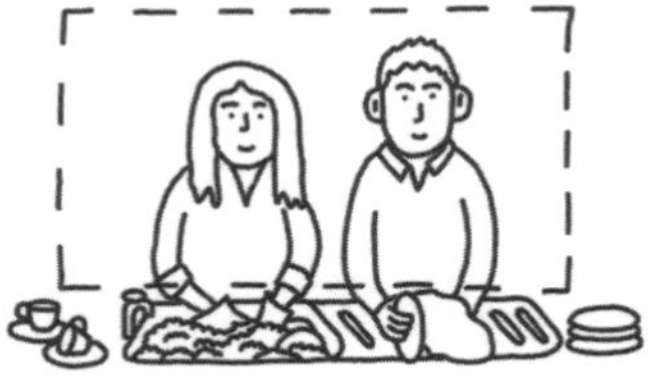

HOUSEHOLD CHORES

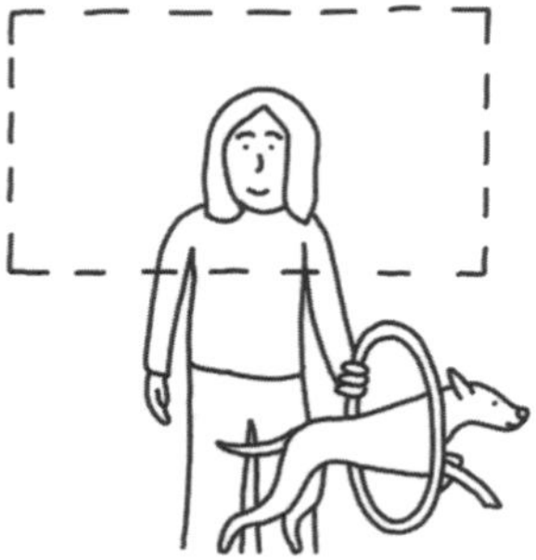

TRAINING ANIMALS

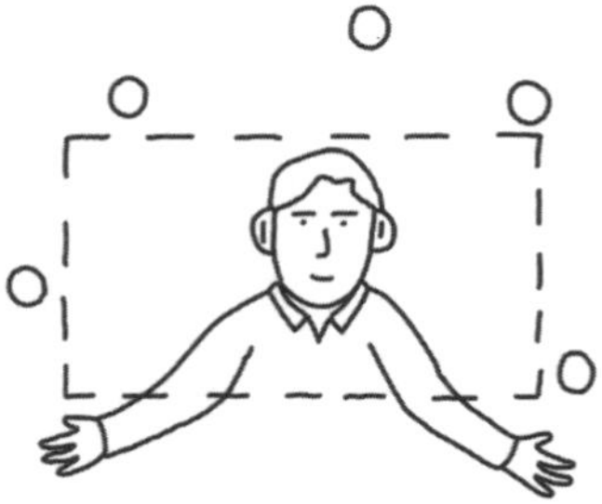

CIRCUS SKILLS (BASIC)

CHURCH BUILDINGS

THEIR USE BY CLERGY DURING LOCKDOWN

MANY OPINIONS HAVE BEEN EXPRESSED...

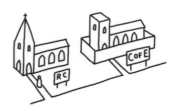

OTHER DENOMINATIONS ARE USING THEIR BUILDINGS

EVERYONE ELSE HAS HAD TO STAY AT HOME, NOT GOING TO PLACES THEY CONSIDER IMPORTANT

I'VE NEVER BEEN ABLE TO USE THE CHURCH BUILDING ANYWAY

WE ARE RETREATING BY BROADCASTING FROM HOME

IS GOD LESS PRESENT HERE →

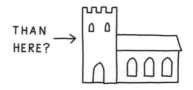

THAN HERE? →

WE DON'T EVEN HAVE A CHURCH BUILDING

ST UNSOUND

WORSHIP TAKING PLACE IN THE BUILDING IS CENTRAL TO MY FAITH

BUT ACTUALLY...

IT TURNS OUT THERE ISN'T A PHONE SIGNAL ANYWAY

LOCKDOWN

WHAT TO DO WITH THE VARIOUS ITEMS OF ANTI-COVID EQUIPMENT DURING THE WEEKS WE HAVE TO STAY AT HOME

PERSPEX SCREENS

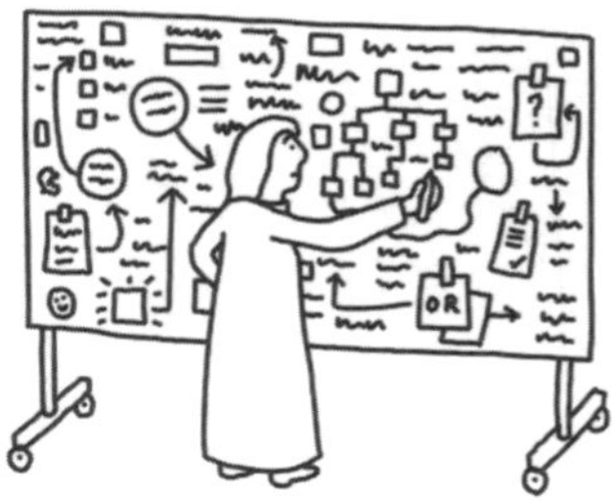
OR

PLANNING SERMONS IN THE STYLE OF FAVOURITE DETECTIVE SERIES

SPRAYS AND GELS

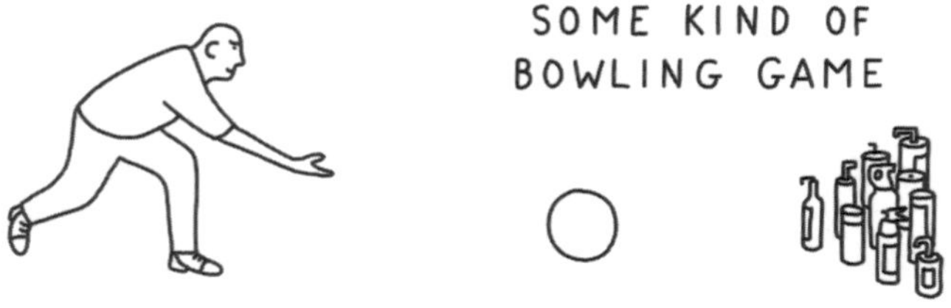

SOME KIND OF BOWLING GAME

SIGNAGE

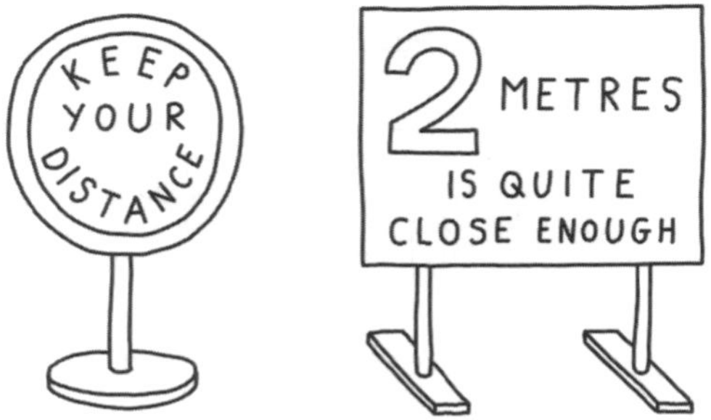
KEEP YOUR DISTANCE
2 METRES IS QUITE CLOSE ENOUGH

USE AT YOUTH GROUP EVENTS IN YEARS TO COME

THE BITS OF THE PEWS WE DON'T NEED

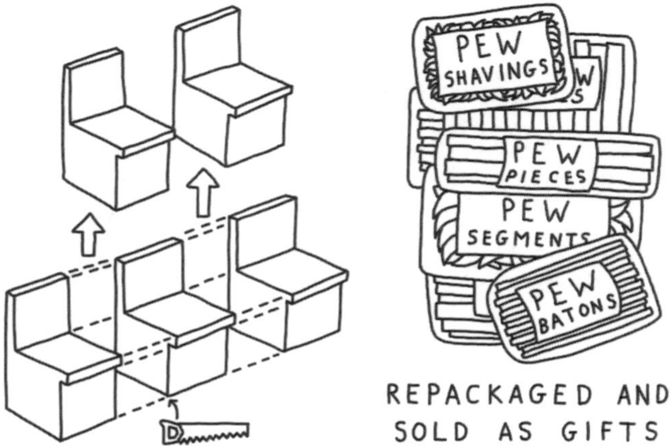
PEW SHAVINGS
PEW PIECES
PEW SEGMENTS
PEW BATONS

REPACKAGED AND SOLD AS GIFTS

THE 12 DAYS OF CHRISTMAS
ADJUSTED FOR LOCKDOWN

[SOME CONCERN OVER THE TERM 'SUBSTANTIAL MEAL']

DAYS 1-7: CONTINUE PRETTY MUCH AS BEFORE

MILKING SHEDS 2-8 →

8 MAIDS A-MILKING ALLOWED TO CARRY ON (ESSENTIAL WORK)

9 LADIES DANCING OVER ZOOM

10 LORDS A-LEAPING (BUT ONLY IF THEY ARE PART OF THE SAME BUBBLE)

11 PIPERS PIPING BEHIND PERSPEX SCREENS

12 DRUMMERS DRUMMING, THEREBY ANNOYING THE LOCKED-DOWN NEIGHBOURS

REOPENING CHURCHES

MATCH THE PERSON TO THE TASK

PEOPLE

IRATE TWEETER

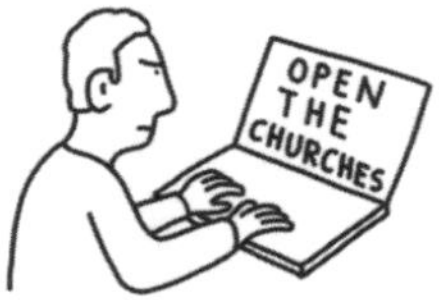
OPEN THE CHURCHES

NEWSPAPER COLUMNIST

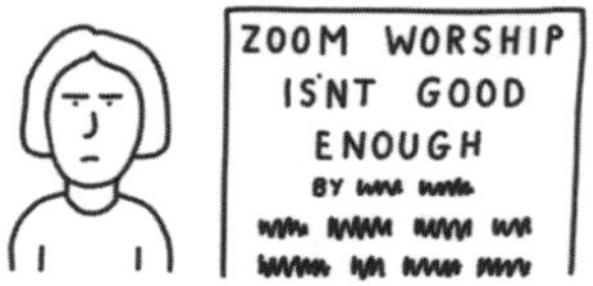
ZOOM WORSHIP ISN'T GOOD ENOUGH

CONCERNED BISHOP

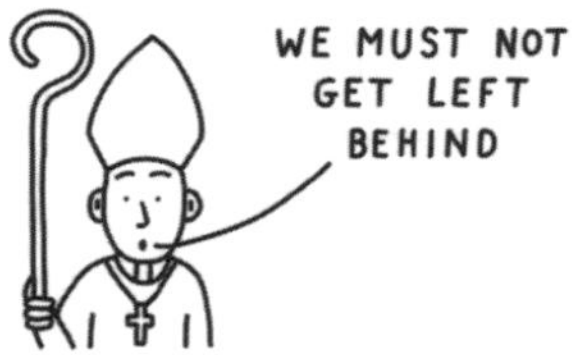
WE MUST NOT GET LEFT BEHIND

LOCAL VICAR

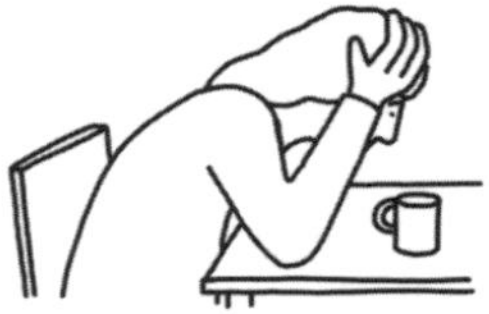

TASKS

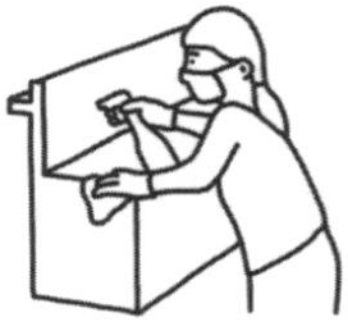

JOINING THE CLEANING ROTA

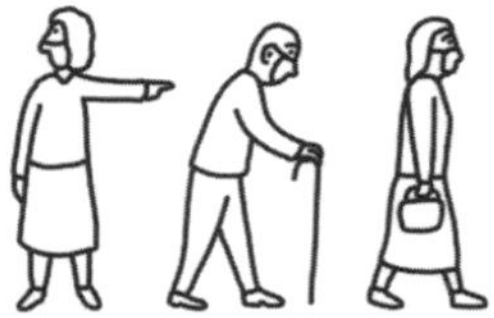

SUPERVISING THE VOLUNTEERS (ALL AGED OVER 70)

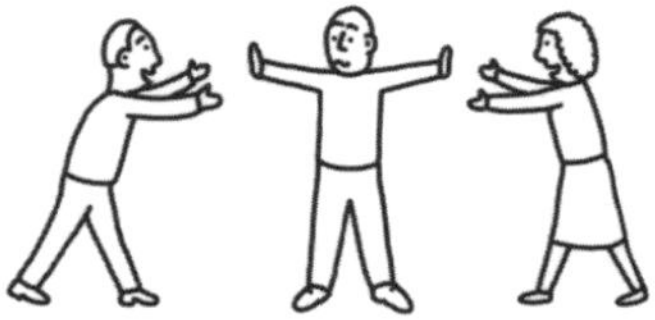

MANAGING THE JOYFULLY NON-COMPLIANT

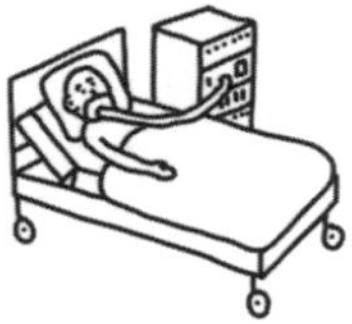

FEELING WEIGHT OF RESPONSIBILITY WHEN IT ALL GOES WRONG

[HINT: THE VICAR WILL HAVE TO DO ALL OF THEM]

TWO METRES

WAYS TO MEASURE IT

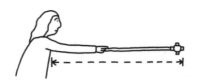

THE LENGTH OF A
WARDEN'S STAVE

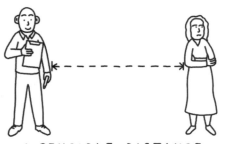

A SENSIBLE DISTANCE
FROM SOMEONE
RECRUITING FOR A ROTA

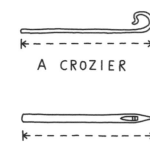

A CROZIER

AN ORGAN PIPE
OF APPROXIMATELY
THAT LENGTH

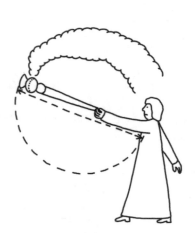

THE DIAMETER OF
THE ARC OF A
SWINGING THURIBLE

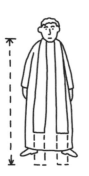

1.3 STOLES

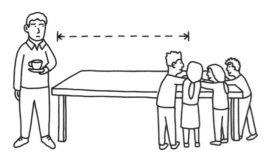

AS CLOSE AS YOU CAN
GET TO THE BISCUITS
WHEN THE CHILDREN'S
GROUP IS RELEASED

BOOKING SEATS

TIPS FOR RESERVING A PEW WHEN SPACE IS LIMITED

MULTIPLE DEVICES

BE READY THE MOMENT BOOKINGS OPEN

8AM IN ABERDEEN?

CAST THE NET WIDE

I CAN DO TWO PRIME BACK-PEW SEATS...

BE PREPARED TO USE UNOFFICIAL CHANNELS

PUT ME DOWN FOR A RICH TEA AND A BOURBON

DON'T FORGET THE HOSPITALITY PACKAGES

EXTENDING YOUR CHURCH

TO FIT MORE PEOPLE IN AT A TWO-METRE DISTANCE FROM EACH OTHER

GAZEBO PORCH-EXTENSIONS

SPREAD OUT INTO THE CAR PARK

KEEP TWO GRAVESTONES APART
1741
1813
1697

CHURCHYARD SERVICES

POST BOX
PHONE BOX
BENCH (RESTRICTED VIEW)
BOLLARD (NOT YET CLAIMED)

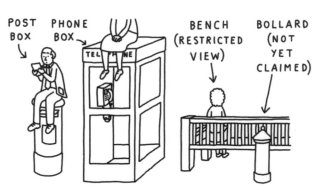

MAKE USE OF STREET FURNITURE

MASKS
SCENES FROM THE 10AM

ASCERTAINING WHETHER ANY OF THE HUMOROUS ASIDES ARE ELICITING A SMILE

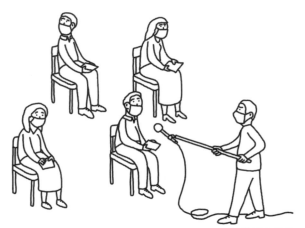

ESTABLISHING WHICH MEMBER
OF THE CONGREGATION
IS SINGING ILLEGALLY

FINDING A PEW THROUGH
MISTED-UP SPECTACLES

FACE MASKS

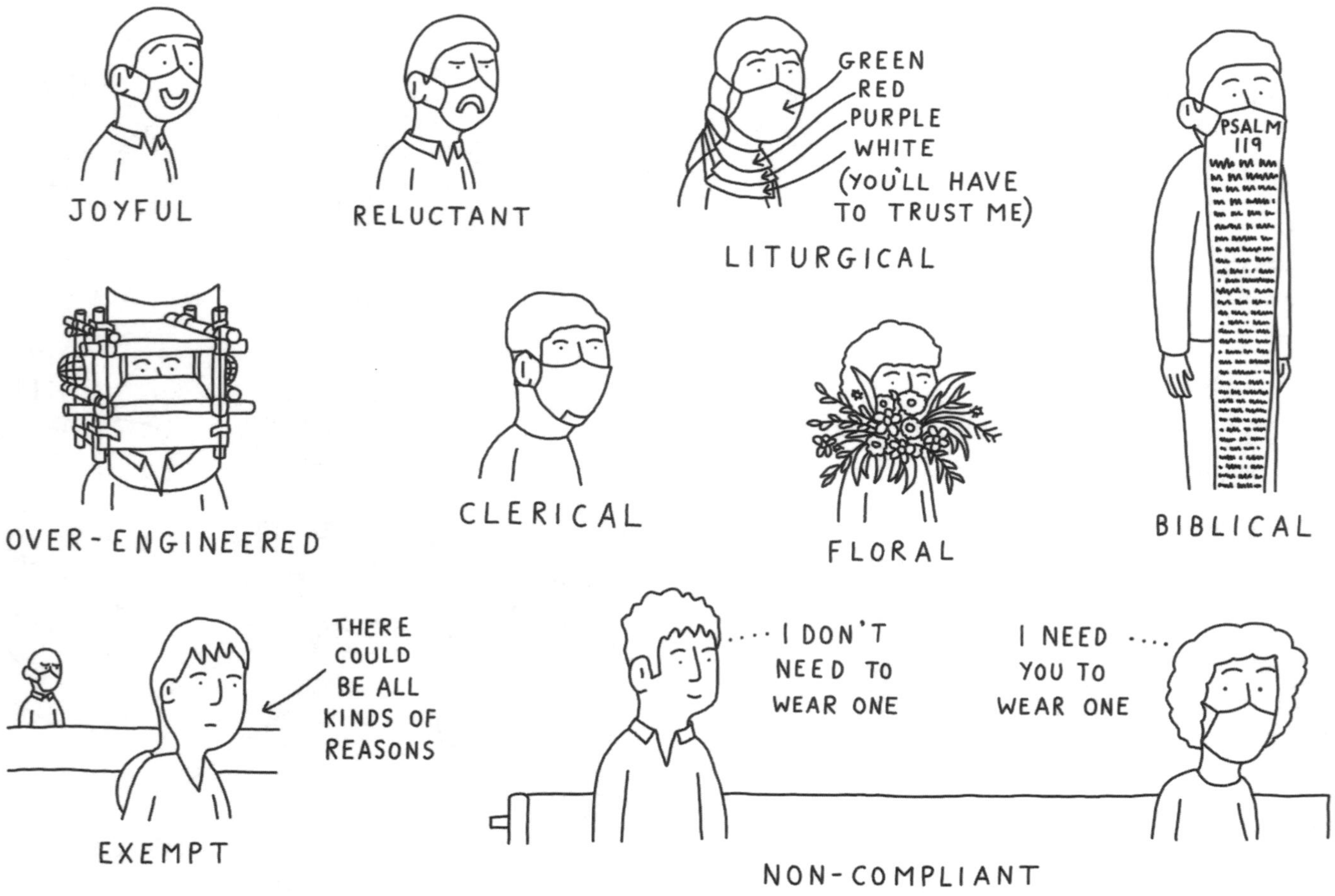
JOYFUL
RELUCTANT
GREEN
RED
PURPLE
WHITE
(YOU'LL HAVE TO TRUST ME)
LITURGICAL
PSALM 119
BIBLICAL
OVER-ENGINEERED
CLERICAL
FLORAL
THERE COULD BE ALL KINDS OF REASONS
EXEMPT
I DON'T NEED TO WEAR ONE
I NEED YOU TO WEAR ONE
NON-COMPLIANT

VENTILATION

WE NEED TO KEEP THE WINDOWS AND DOORS OPEN

BENEFITS

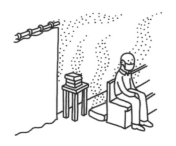

EASING THE MUSTY SMELL

OOH... IS THAT A SERMON?

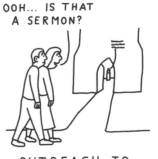

OUTREACH TO PASSERS-BY

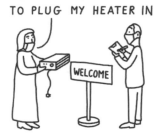

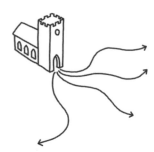

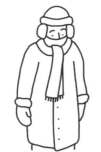

A RELAXING OF THE DRESS CODE

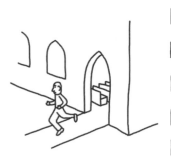

IT'S EASY TO LEAVE QUICKLY

DRAWBACKS

I'LL NEED SOMEWHERE TO PLUG MY HEATER IN
WELCOME

IT IS A BIT CHILLY

THE CONGREGATION MIGHT WANDER OFF

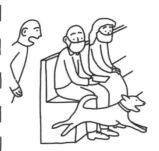

UNEXPECTED VISITORS

&$@✱#!

ADDITIONS TO THE LITURGY FROM OUTSIDE

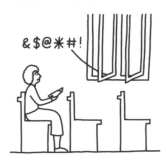

OBSCURED VIEWS

IN THE CHURCH BUILDING

THE SHEER QUANTITY OF LIVESTREAMING EQUIPMENT

OVERZEALOUS STEWARDING

WATCHING FROM HOME

WELC TO
THIS MO NG'S
SERVI ROM
ST 'S

DOMESTIC OBSTRUCTIONS

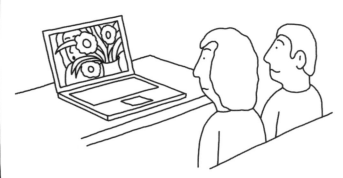

PROBLEMS AT THE OTHER END

SIGNAGE

DURING A PANDEMIC

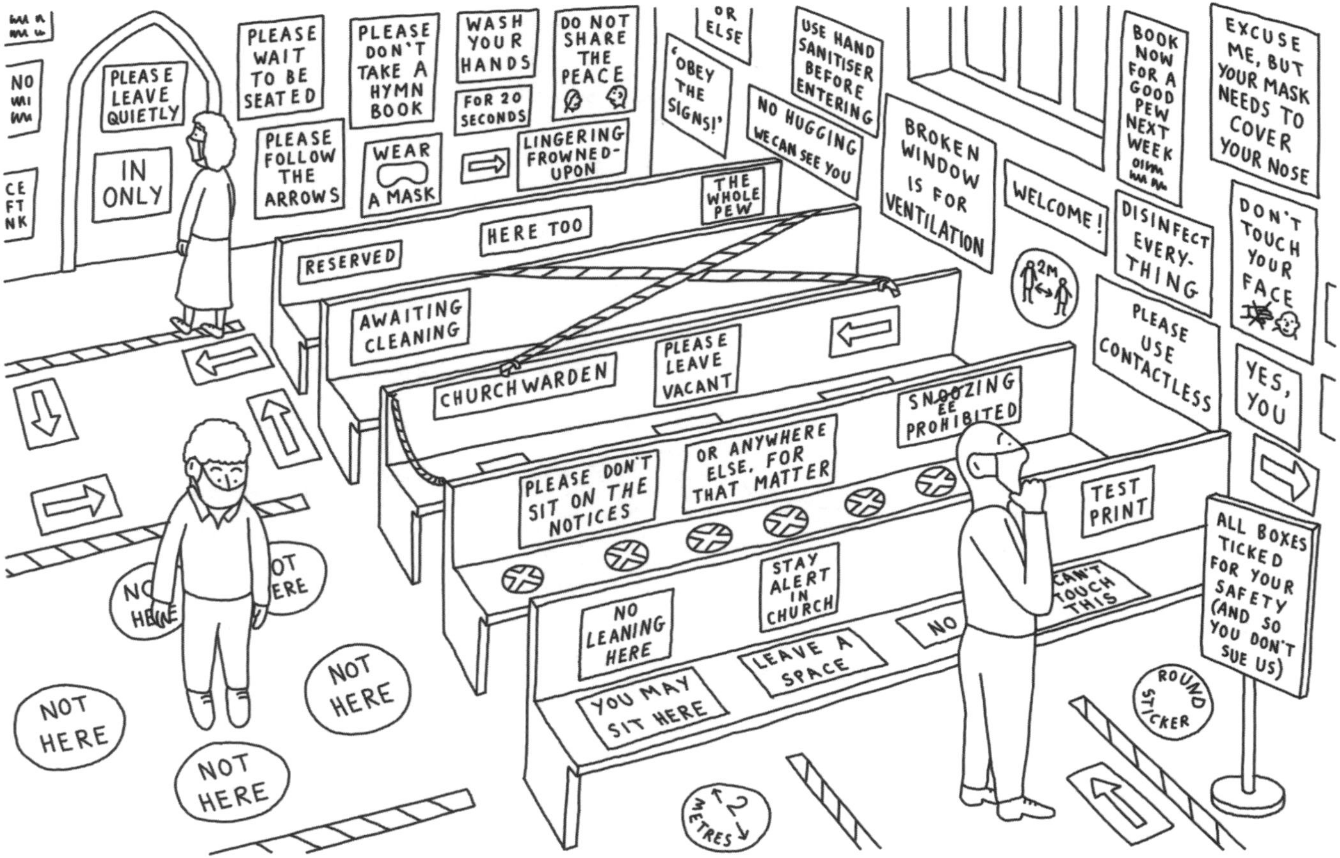
PLEASE LEAVE QUIETLY
IN ONLY
PLEASE WAIT TO BE SEATED
PLEASE DON'T TAKE A HYMN BOOK
WASH YOUR HANDS
FOR 20 SECONDS
DO NOT SHARE THE PEACE
PLEASE FOLLOW THE ARROWS
WEAR A MASK
LINGERING FROWNED-UPON
OR ELSE
'OBEY THE SIGNS!'
USE HAND SANITISER BEFORE ENTERING
NO HUGGING
WE CAN SEE YOU
BROKEN WINDOW IS FOR VENTILATION
BOOK NOW FOR A GOOD PEW NEXT WEEK
EXCUSE ME, BUT YOUR MASK NEEDS TO COVER YOUR NOSE
WELCOME!
DISINFECT EVERY-THING
DON'T TOUCH YOUR FACE
2M
PLEASE USE CONTACTLESS
YES, YOU
THE WHOLE PEW
HERE TOO
RESERVED
AWAITING CLEANING
CHURCHWARDEN
PLEASE LEAVE VACANT
SNOOZING PROHIBITED
PLEASE DON'T SIT ON THE NOTICES
OR ANYWHERE ELSE, FOR THAT MATTER
TEST PRINT
ALL BOXES TICKED FOR YOUR SAFETY (AND SO YOU DON'T SUE US)
NO LEANING HERE
STAY ALERT IN CHURCH
CAN'T TOUCH THIS
NO
LEAVE A SPACE
YOU MAY SIT HERE
ROUND STICKER
2 METRES
NOT HERE
NOT HERE
NOT HERE
NOT HERE
NOT HERE
NOT HERE

STICKS

RECOGNITION GUIDE

← BISHOP'S CROZIER

DRAWN FROM MEMORY, HAVING NOT BEEN SEEN FOR A WHILE

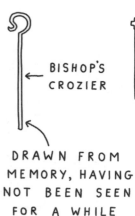

← WANDS, STAVES, VERGES

LOOK THESE UP IF UNCERTAIN

THE YOUTH GROUP POOL CUE

PLAQUE COMMEMORATING BLESSING OF THE CUE, 1987

← THIS ONE, KEPT IN THE VESTRY, WHICH MIGHT BE SOMETHING TO DO WITH OPENING THE HIGH WINDOWS, BUT WE CAN'T QUITE REMEMBER

BRIAN WILL KNOW

CURRENT USES

SHAKING HANDS

ENFORCING SOCIAL DISTANCING

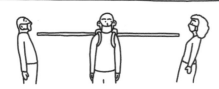

ALERTING TRANSGRESSORS TO THEIR FOLLY

ASSISTING WITH BAPTISMS

SKILLS

EXPERTISE GAINED DURING LOCKDOWN		HOW THESE NEW-FOUND ABILITIES CAN BE PUT TO USE WHEN THE CHURCH REOPENS
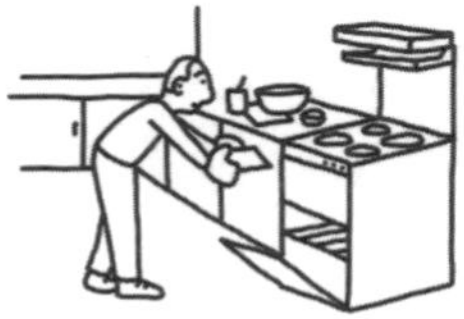	MAKING THINGS IN THE KITCHEN →	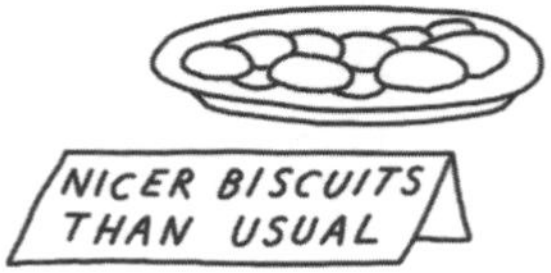NICER BISCUITS THAN USUAL
[3 WEEKS EARLIER THAN USUAL] 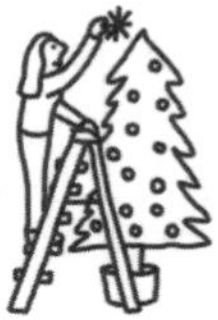	DIY TASKS/ WORKING AT HEIGHTS →	WE NEED A VOLUNTEER TO GO UP AND ADJUST THE SPIRE 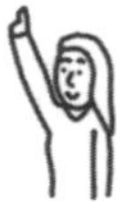
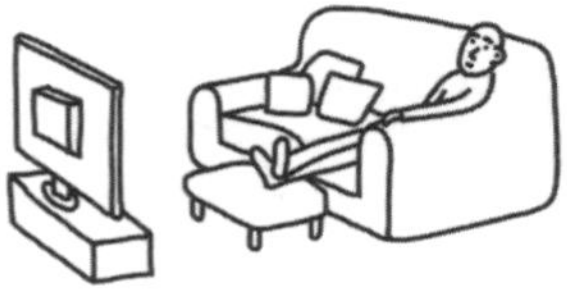	SITTING AROUND WATCHING TV →	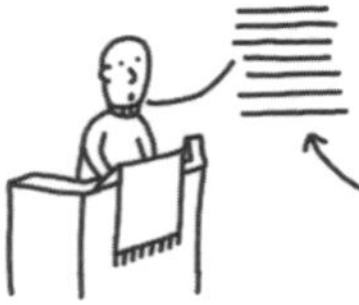 BOX-SET-INSPIRED PROFOUND INSIGHT
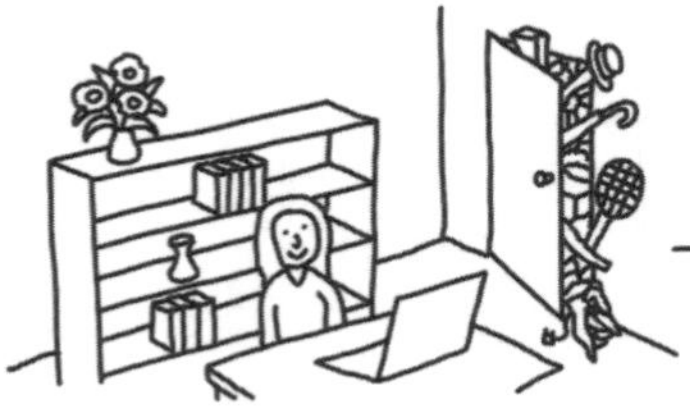	APPEARING AS IF EVERYTHING IS FINE →	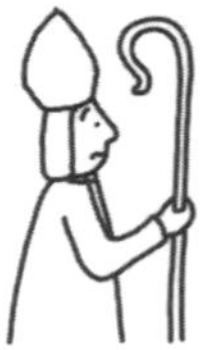 THERE'S VERY LITTLE TO SEE IN HERE, BISHOP... 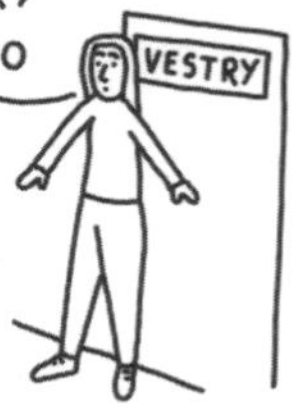VESTRY

BEATITUDES

FOR A GLOBAL PANDEMIC

BLESSED ARE THOSE
WHO STAY INDOORS

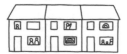

FOR THEY HAVE
PROTECTED OTHERS

BLESSED ARE THE
UNEMPLOYED AND THE
SELF-EMPLOYED

FOR THEIR NEED OF
GOD IS GREAT

BLESSED ARE THE
CORNER SHOPKEEPERS

FOR THEY ARE THE
PURVEYORS OF SCARCE
THINGS

BLESSED ARE THE DELIVERY
DRIVERS AND THE POSTAL
WORKERS

FOR THEY ARE THE
BRINGERS OF ESSENTIAL
THINGS

BLESSED ARE THE HOSPITAL
WORKERS; THE AMBULANCE CREWS,
THE DOCTORS, THE NURSES, THE CARE
ASSISTANTS, AND THE CLEANERS

FOR THEY STAND BETWEEN US AND
THE GRAVE, AND THE KINGDOM OF
HEAVEN IS SURELY THEIRS

BLESSED ARE THE
CHECKOUT WORKERS

FOR THEY HAVE PATIENCE AND
FORTITUDE IN THE FACE OF
OVERWORK AND FRUSTRATION

BLESSED ARE THE
REFUSE COLLECTORS

FOR THEY WILL SEE
GOD DESPITE THE
MOUNTAINS OF WASTE

BLESSED ARE THE
TEACHERS

FOR THEY REMAIN
STEADFAST AND
CONSTANT IN
DISTURBING TIMES

BLESSED ARE THE CHURCH
WORKERS; THE DEACONS,
PRIESTS AND BISHOPS

FOR THEY ARE A COMFORTING
PRESENCE IN A HURTING
WORLD AS THEY CONTINUE TO
SIGNPOST TOWARDS GOD

BLESSED ARE THE SINGLE
PARENTS,

FOR THEY ARE COPING
ALONE WITH THEIR
RESPONSIBILITIES AND
THERE IS NO RESPITE

BLESSED ARE THOSE WHO
ARE ALONE,

FOR THEY ARE CHILDREN OF
GOD AND WITH HIM THEY
WILL NEVER BE LONELY

BLESSED ARE THE
BEREAVED,

FOR WHOM THE WORST HAS
ALREADY HAPPENED. THEY
SHALL BE COMFORTED

BLESSED ARE THOSE WHO
ARE ISOLATED WITH THEIR
ABUSERS

FOR ONE DAY - WE PRAY-
THEY WILL KNOW SAFETY

BLESSED ARE ALL DURING THIS TIME WHO HAVE PURE HEARTS;
ALL WHO STILL HUNGER AND THIRST FOR JUSTICE; ALL WHO
WORK FOR PEACE AND WHO MODEL MERCY

MAY YOU KNOW COMFORT. MAY YOU KNOW CALM. AND MAY THE
GRACE OF OUR LORD JESUS CHRIST, AND THE LOVE OF GOD, AND
THE FELLOWSHIP OF THE HOLY SPIRIT, BE WITH US ALL. AMEN

PART THREE: THE CHURCH YEAR, LOOKING FORWARD

THE CHURCH YEAR

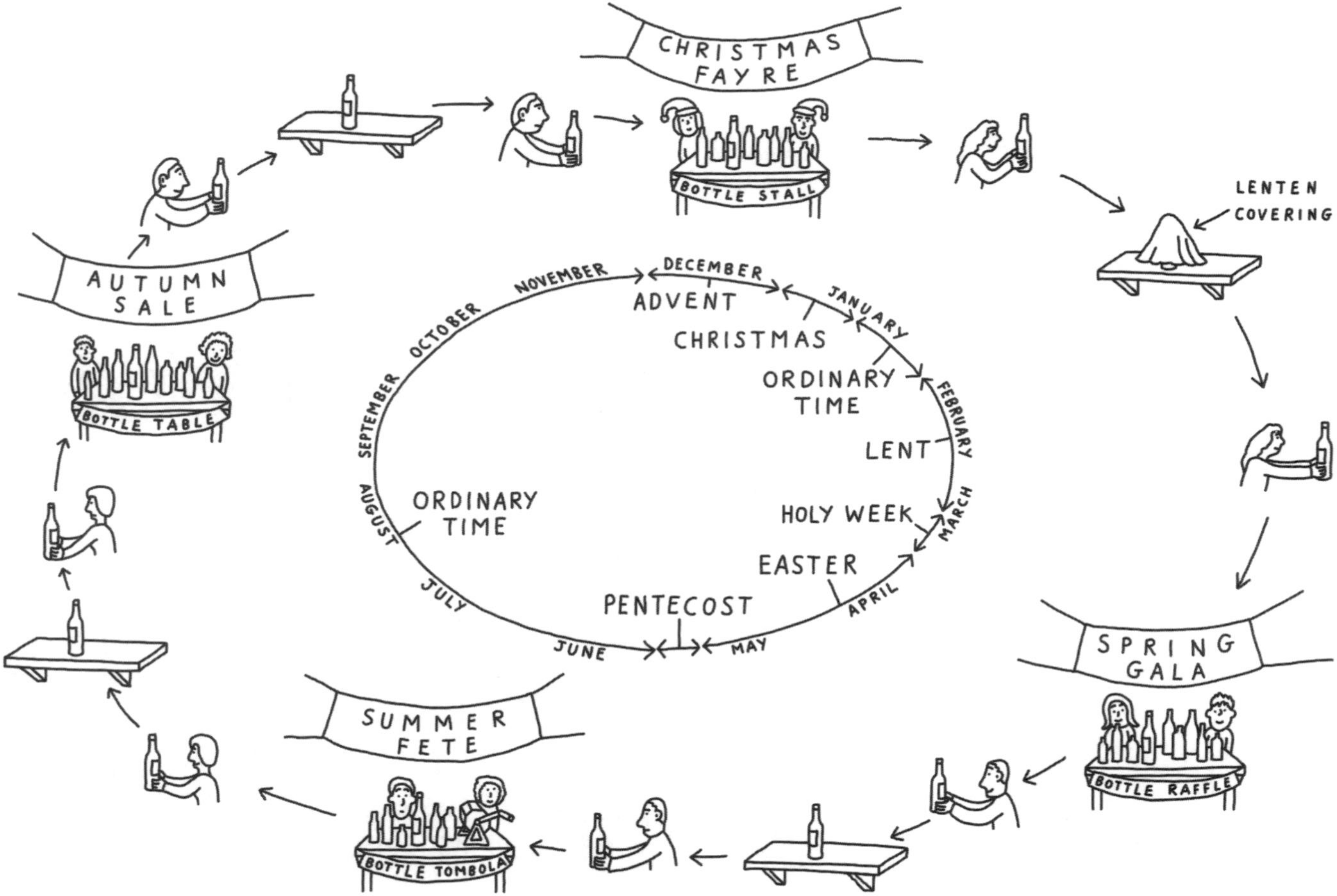
CHRISTMAS FAYRE
BOTTLE STALL
LENTEN COVERING
SPRING GALA
BOTTLE RAFFLE
SUMMER FETE
BOTTLE TOMBOLA
AUTUMN SALE
BOTTLE TABLE
DECEMBER
ADVENT
JANUARY
CHRISTMAS
ORDINARY TIME
FEBRUARY
LENT
MARCH
HOLY WEEK
EASTER
APRIL
MAY
PENTECOST
JUNE
JULY
AUGUST
ORDINARY TIME
SEPTEMBER
OCTOBER
NOVEMBER

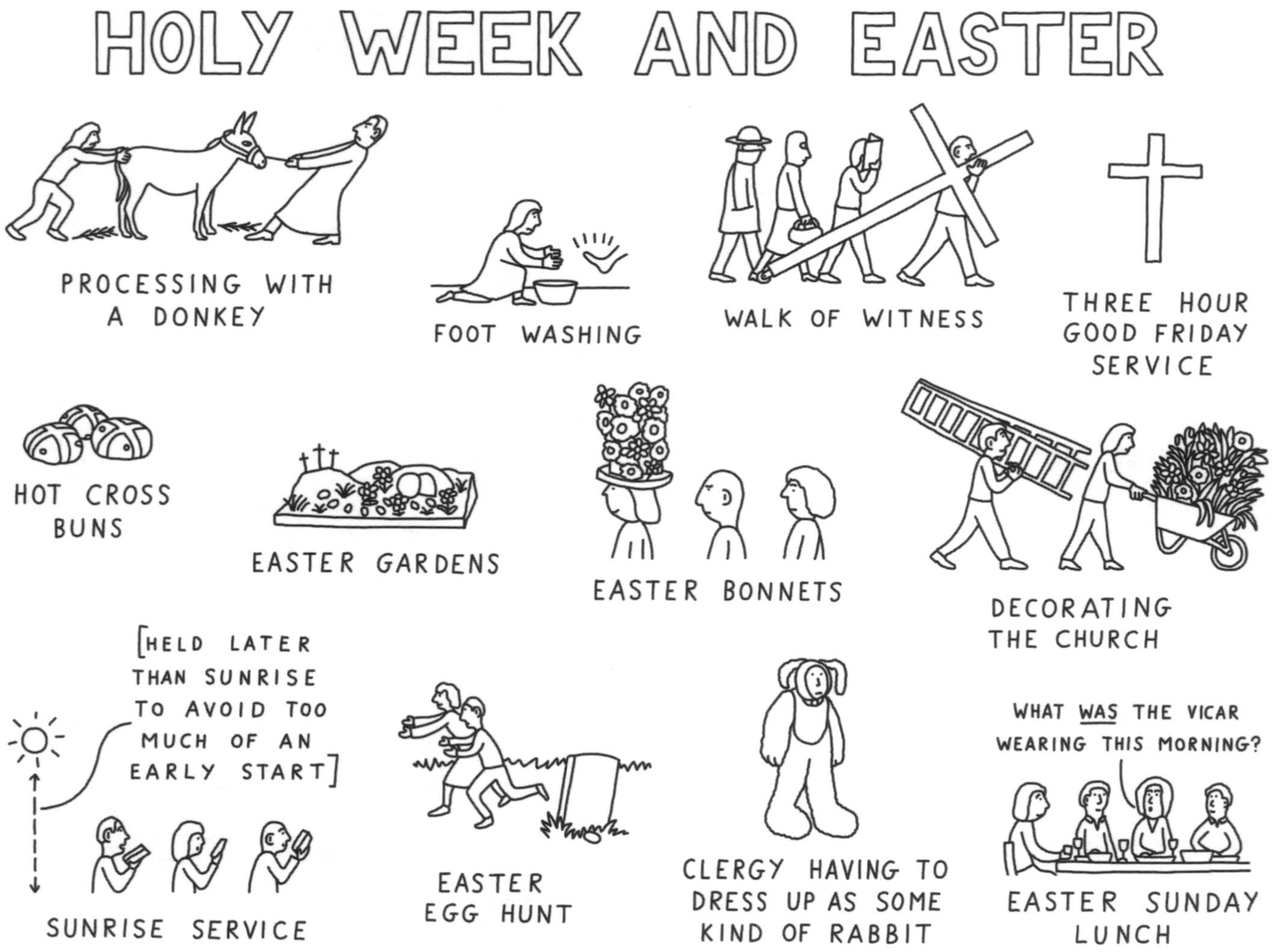
HOLY WEEK AND EASTER
PROCESSING WITH A DONKEY
FOOT WASHING
WALK OF WITNESS
THREE HOUR GOOD FRIDAY SERVICE
HOT CROSS BUNS
EASTER GARDENS
EASTER BONNETS
DECORATING THE CHURCH
[HELD LATER THAN SUNRISE TO AVOID TOO MUCH OF AN EARLY START]
SUNRISE SERVICE
EASTER EGG HUNT
CLERGY HAVING TO DRESS UP AS SOME KIND OF RABBIT
WHAT WAS THE VICAR WEARING THIS MORNING?
EASTER SUNDAY LUNCH

(2019 version of the cartoon)

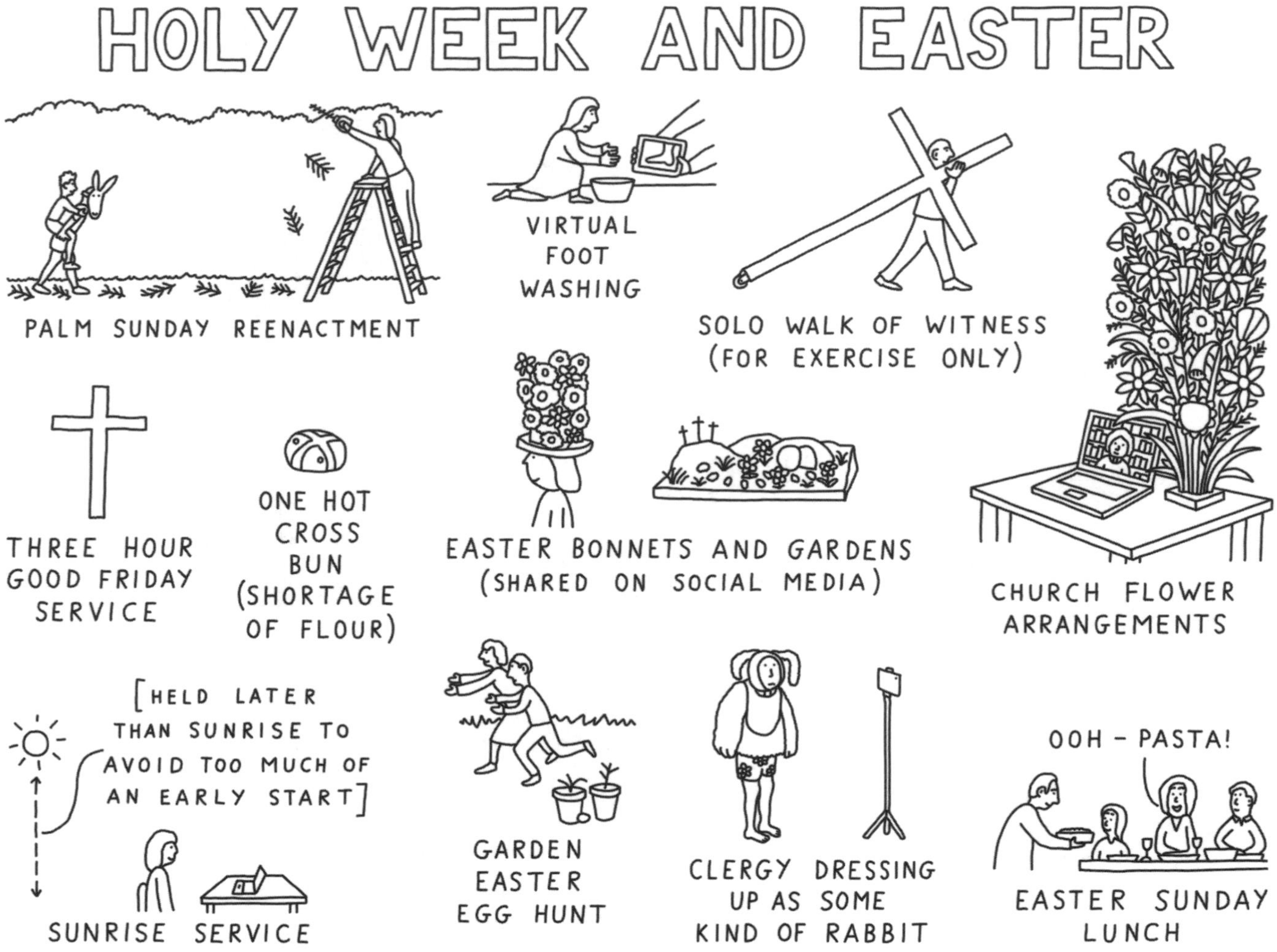

HOLY WEEK AND EASTER

PALM SUNDAY REENACTMENT

VIRTUAL FOOT WASHING

SOLO WALK OF WITNESS (FOR EXERCISE ONLY)

THREE HOUR GOOD FRIDAY SERVICE

ONE HOT CROSS BUN (SHORTAGE OF FLOUR)

EASTER BONNETS AND GARDENS (SHARED ON SOCIAL MEDIA)

CHURCH FLOWER ARRANGEMENTS

[HELD LATER THAN SUNRISE TO AVOID TOO MUCH OF AN EARLY START]

SUNRISE SERVICE

GARDEN EASTER EGG HUNT

CLERGY DRESSING UP AS SOME KIND OF RABBIT

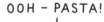

OOH - PASTA!

EASTER SUNDAY LUNCH

(2020 version of the cartoon)

THE EASTER SERVICE

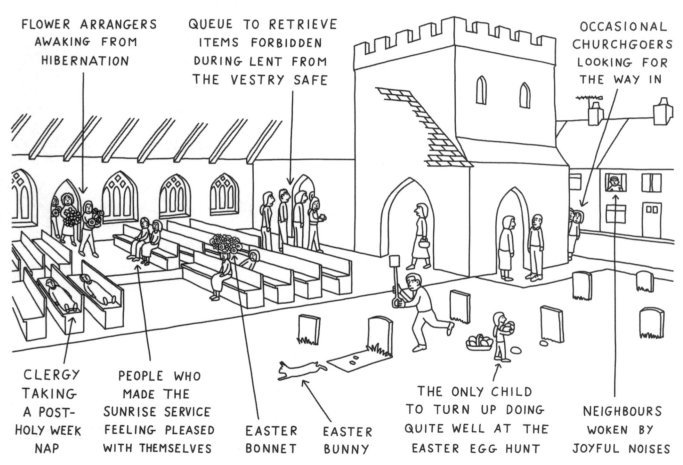

FLOWER ARRANGERS AWAKING FROM HIBERNATION

QUEUE TO RETRIEVE ITEMS FORBIDDEN DURING LENT FROM THE VESTRY SAFE

OCCASIONAL CHURCHGOERS LOOKING FOR THE WAY IN

CLERGY TAKING A POST-HOLY WEEK NAP

PEOPLE WHO MADE THE SUNRISE SERVICE FEELING PLEASED WITH THEMSELVES

EASTER BONNET

EASTER BUNNY

THE ONLY CHILD TO TURN UP DOING QUITE WELL AT THE EASTER EGG HUNT

NEIGHBOURS WOKEN BY JOYFUL NOISES

PENTECOST
VARIOUS HAZARDS

BEING DAZZLED BY
BRIGHT CLOTHING

OVERENTHUSIASTIC
HALLELUJAHS

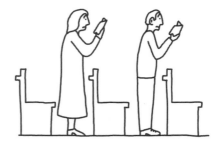

CONSTERNATION AT
SONGS CONTAINING THE
WORDS 'JOY' OR 'DANCE'

ILL-ADVISED
REENACTMENTS

ERRANT
DOVES

TECHNOLOGY

HOW IT CAN BE USED TO COVER SUMMER ABSENCES

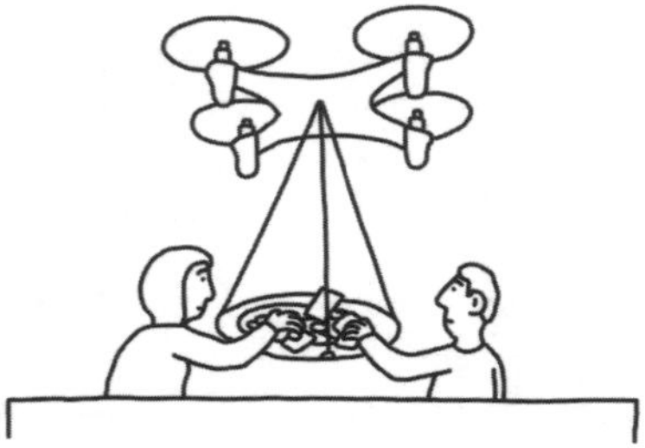

COLLECTION BY DRONE

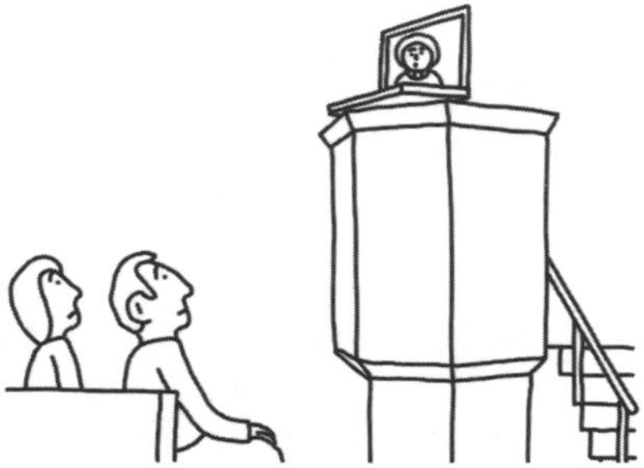

PRERECORDED SERMONS

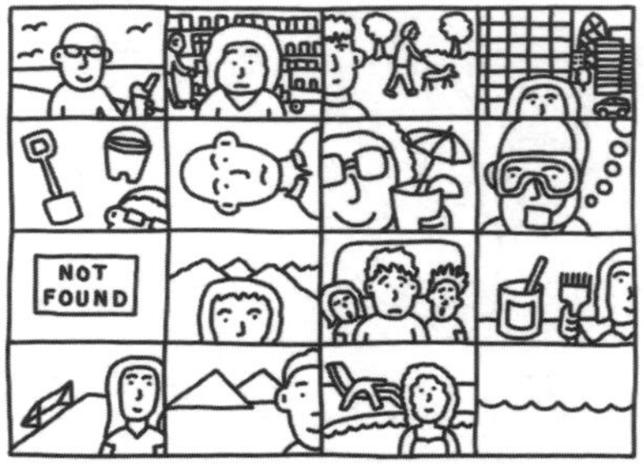
NOT FOUND

P.C.C. MEETINGS BY CONFERENCE CALL

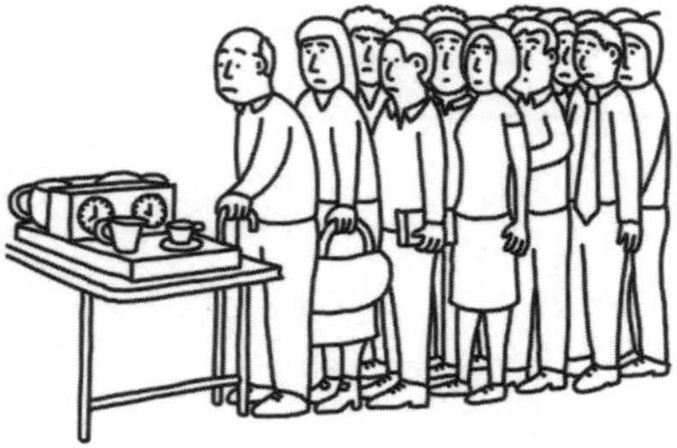

POST-SERVICE DRINKS PROVIDED BY A TEASMADE

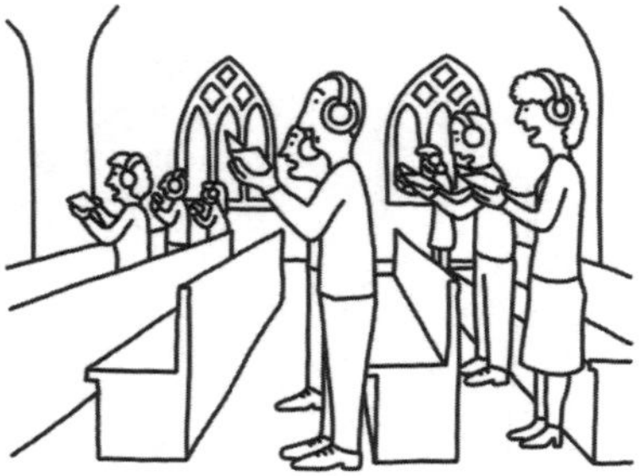

INDIVIDUALLY-TAILORED HYMN CHOICES USING A MUSIC-STREAMING WEBSITE

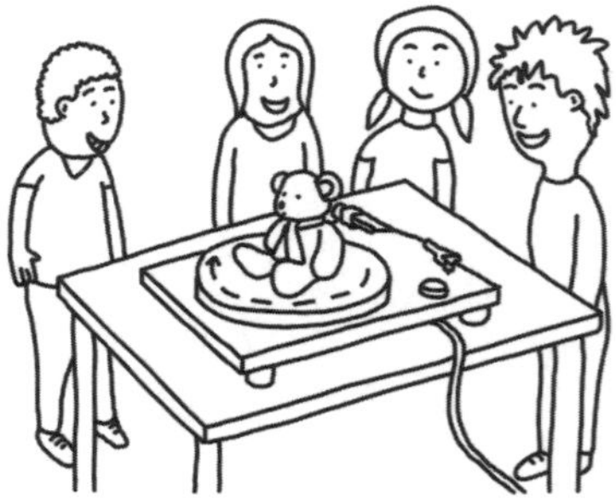

KEEPING THE SUNDAY SCHOOL AMUSED WITH A BEAR ON A RECORD PLAYER

THE WEDDING
THE COUPLE HAVE SOME REQUIREMENTS

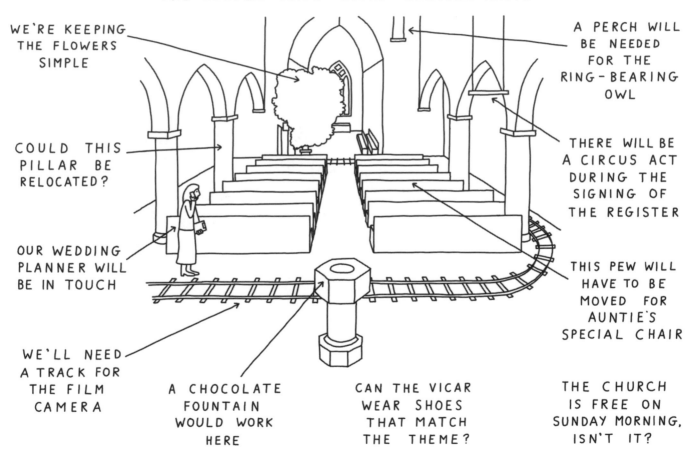

WE'RE KEEPING THE FLOWERS SIMPLE

A PERCH WILL BE NEEDED FOR THE RING-BEARING OWL

COULD THIS PILLAR BE RELOCATED?

THERE WILL BE A CIRCUS ACT DURING THE SIGNING OF THE REGISTER

OUR WEDDING PLANNER WILL BE IN TOUCH

THIS PEW WILL HAVE TO BE MOVED FOR AUNTIE'S SPECIAL CHAIR

WE'LL NEED A TRACK FOR THE FILM CAMERA

A CHOCOLATE FOUNTAIN WOULD WORK HERE

CAN THE VICAR WEAR SHOES THAT MATCH THE THEME?

THE CHURCH IS FREE ON SUNDAY MORNING, ISN'T IT?

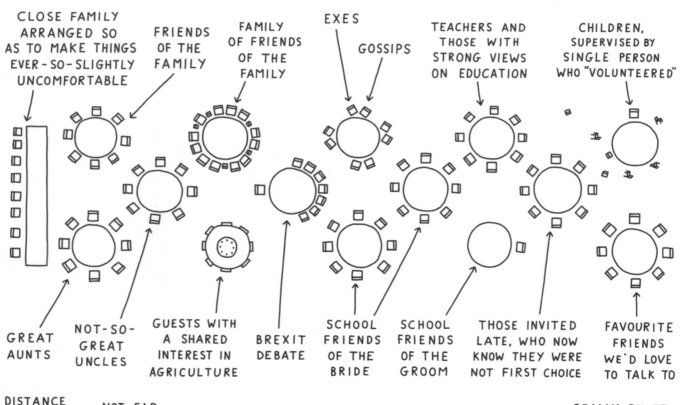

THE WEDDING RECEPTION

THE SEATING PLAN

CLOSE FAMILY ARRANGED SO AS TO MAKE THINGS EVER-SO-SLIGHTLY UNCOMFORTABLE

FRIENDS OF THE FAMILY

FAMILY OF FRIENDS OF THE FAMILY

EXES

GOSSIPS

TEACHERS AND THOSE WITH STRONG VIEWS ON EDUCATION

CHILDREN, SUPERVISED BY SINGLE PERSON WHO "VOLUNTEERED"

GREAT AUNTS

NOT-SO-GREAT UNCLES

GUESTS WITH A SHARED INTEREST IN AGRICULTURE

BREXIT DEBATE

SCHOOL FRIENDS OF THE BRIDE

SCHOOL FRIENDS OF THE GROOM

THOSE INVITED LATE, WHO NOW KNOW THEY WERE NOT FIRST CHOICE

FAVOURITE FRIENDS WE'D LOVE TO TALK TO

DISTANCE FROM COUPLE:

NOT FAR AWAY AT ALL — — — — — — — — — — — — — — → REALLY QUITE SOME WAY AWAY

CRICKET

FIELDING POSITIONS, AND THEIR ECCLESIASTICAL EQUIVALENTS

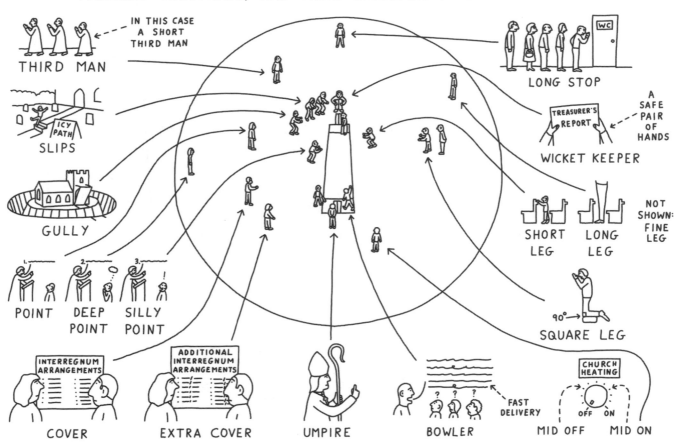

THIRD MAN — IN THIS CASE A SHORT THIRD MAN

SLIPS — ICY PATH

GULLY

POINT   DEEP POINT   SILLY POINT

COVER — INTERREGNUM ARRANGEMENTS

EXTRA COVER — ADDITIONAL INTERREGNUM ARRANGEMENTS

UMPIRE

BOWLER — FAST DELIVERY

MID OFF   MID ON — CHURCH HEATING   OFF   ON

LONG STOP — WC

WICKET KEEPER — TREASURER'S REPORT — A SAFE PAIR OF HANDS

SHORT LEG   LONG LEG   NOT SHOWN: FINE LEG

SQUARE LEG — 90°

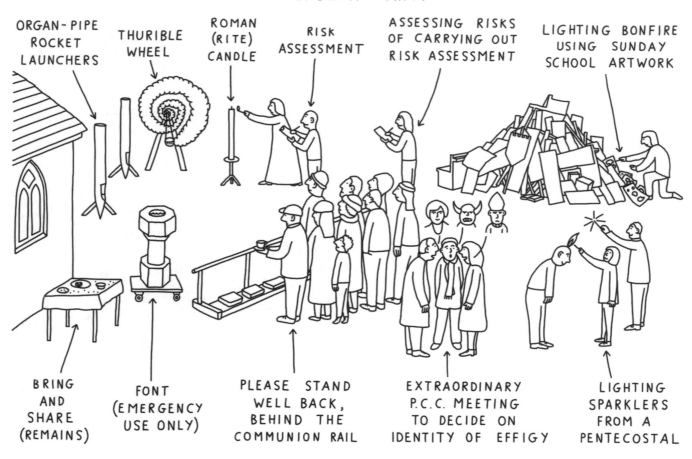

FIREWORKS
THE CHURCH PARTY

ORGAN-PIPE ROCKET LAUNCHERS

THURIBLE WHEEL

ROMAN (RITE) CANDLE

RISK ASSESSMENT

ASSESSING RISKS OF CARRYING OUT RISK ASSESSMENT

LIGHTING BONFIRE USING SUNDAY SCHOOL ARTWORK

BRING AND SHARE (REMAINS)

FONT (EMERGENCY USE ONLY)

PLEASE STAND WELL BACK, BEHIND THE COMMUNION RAIL

EXTRAORDINARY P.C.C. MEETING TO DECIDE ON IDENTITY OF EFFIGY

LIGHTING SPARKLERS FROM A PENTECOSTAL

82

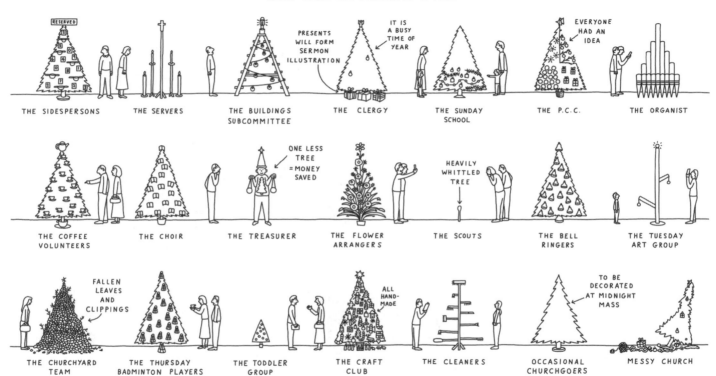

THE CHRISTMAS TREE FESTIVAL

EVERY GROUP HAS DECORATED A TREE

THE SIDESPERSONS

THE SERVERS

THE BUILDINGS SUBCOMMITTEE

PRESENTS WILL FORM SERMON ILLUSTRATION

THE CLERGY

IT IS A BUSY TIME OF YEAR

THE SUNDAY SCHOOL

THE P.C.C.

EVERYONE HAD AN IDEA

THE ORGANIST

THE COFFEE VOLUNTEERS

THE CHOIR

THE TREASURER

ONE LESS TREE = MONEY SAVED

THE FLOWER ARRANGERS

THE SCOUTS

HEAVILY WHITTLED TREE

THE BELL RINGERS

THE TUESDAY ART GROUP

THE CHURCHYARD TEAM

FALLEN LEAVES AND CLIPPINGS

THE THURSDAY BADMINTON PLAYERS

THE TODDLER GROUP

THE CRAFT CLUB

ALL HAND-MADE

THE CLEANERS

OCCASIONAL CHURCHGOERS

TO BE DECORATED AT MIDNIGHT MASS

MESSY CHURCH

83

THE NATIVITY

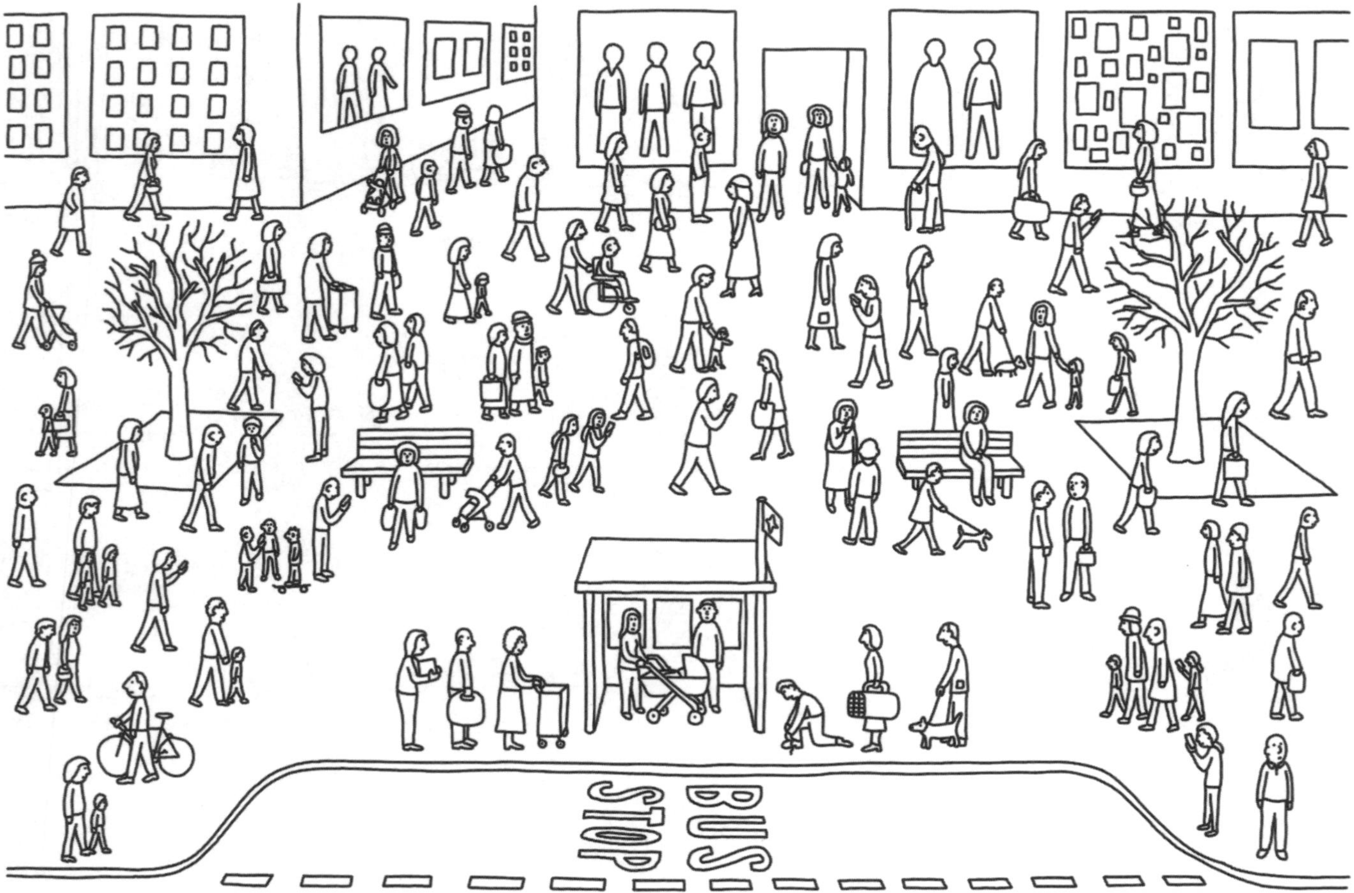
BUS
STOP

THE FIRST SERVICE

AFTER SEVERAL MONTHS AWAY

LOCKDOWN HAIRSTYLES

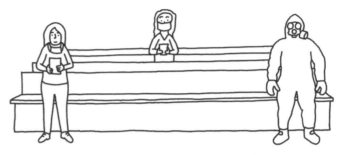

A VARIETY OF LEVELS OF COMMITMENT TO MASK-WEARING

YOU'RE SUPPOSED TO PUT IT IN, NOT TAKE IT OUT!

PEOPLE WHO HAVE FORGOTTEN THE WAY WE DO THINGS

THOSE WHOSE ONLY INTERACTIONS HAVE BEEN VIA ZOOM

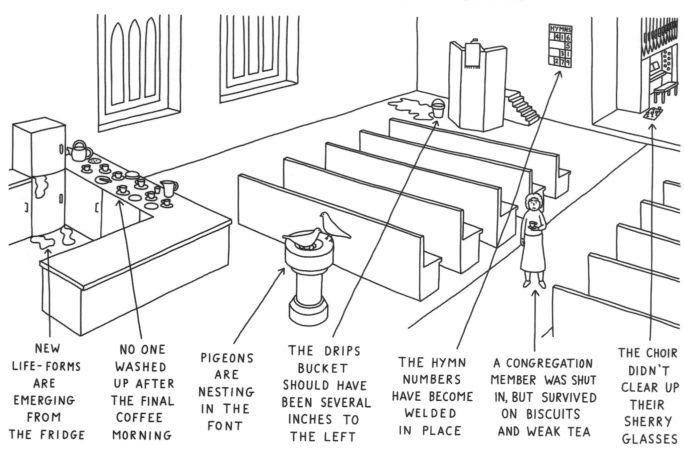

DISCOVERIES

MADE UPON RETURNING TO THE CHURCH BUILDING

NEW LIFE-FORMS ARE EMERGING FROM THE FRIDGE

NO ONE WASHED UP AFTER THE FINAL COFFEE MORNING

PIGEONS ARE NESTING IN THE FONT

THE DRIPS BUCKET SHOULD HAVE BEEN SEVERAL INCHES TO THE LEFT

THE HYMN NUMBERS HAVE BECOME WELDED IN PLACE

A CONGREGATION MEMBER WAS SHUT IN, BUT SURVIVED ON BISCUITS AND WEAK TEA

THE CHOIR DIDN'T CLEAR UP THEIR SHERRY GLASSES

GOING BACK TO CHURCH

THINGS TO REMEMBER

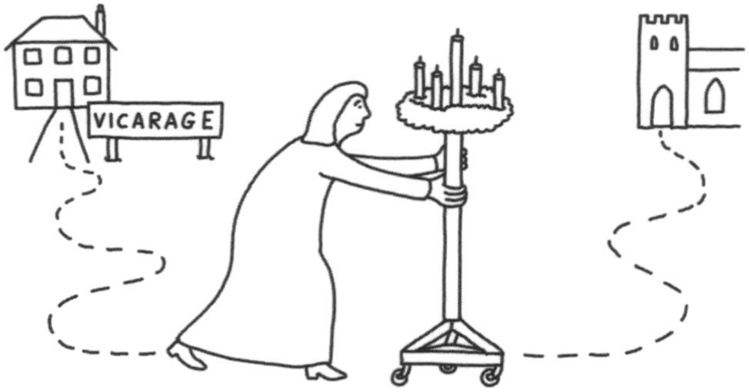
VICARAGE

THE CURRENT STATUS OF THE ADVENT WREATH

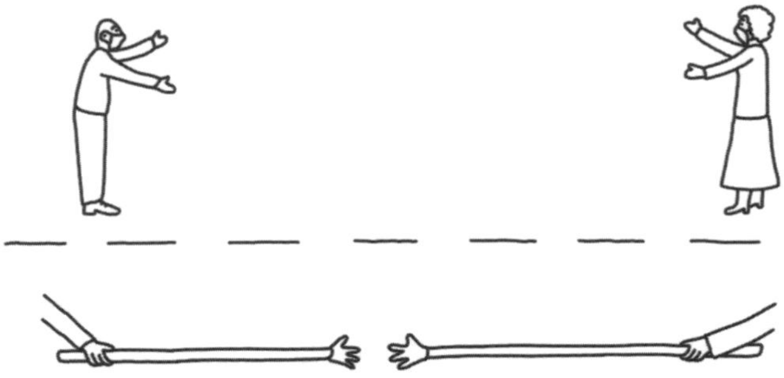

HOW TO GREET PEOPLE

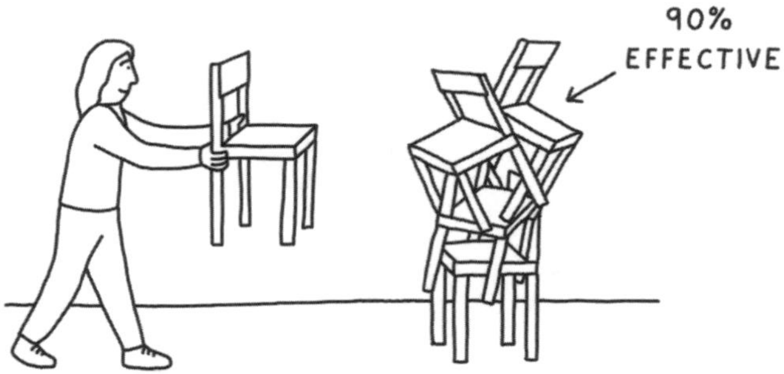
90%
EFFECTIVE

THE BEST WAY TO UNDERTAKE REGULAR TASKS

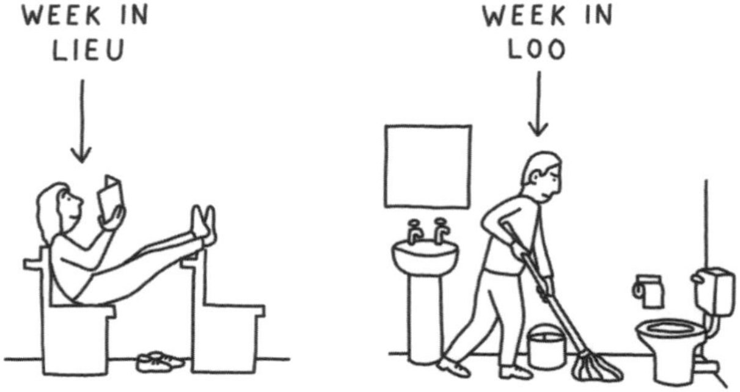
WEEK IN
LIEU
WEEK IN
LOO

WHERE WE'RE UP TO ON THE ROTAS

ARRIVING AT CHURCH

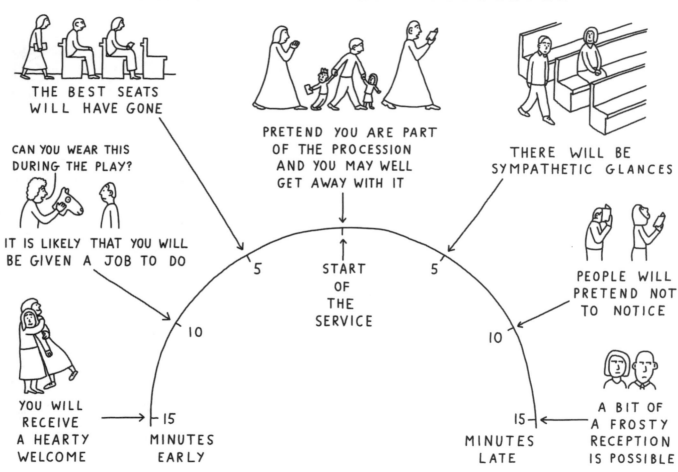

THE BEST SEATS WILL HAVE GONE

CAN YOU WEAR THIS DURING THE PLAY?

IT IS LIKELY THAT YOU WILL BE GIVEN A JOB TO DO

PRETEND YOU ARE PART OF THE PROCESSION AND YOU MAY WELL GET AWAY WITH IT

THERE WILL BE SYMPATHETIC GLANCES

PEOPLE WILL PRETEND NOT TO NOTICE

YOU WILL RECEIVE A HEARTY WELCOME

5

START OF THE SERVICE

5

10

10

15 MINUTES EARLY

15 MINUTES LATE

A BIT OF A FROSTY RECEPTION IS POSSIBLE

THE OPEN CHURCH

HOW TO SPEND THE TIME WHEN YOU'RE ON DUTY

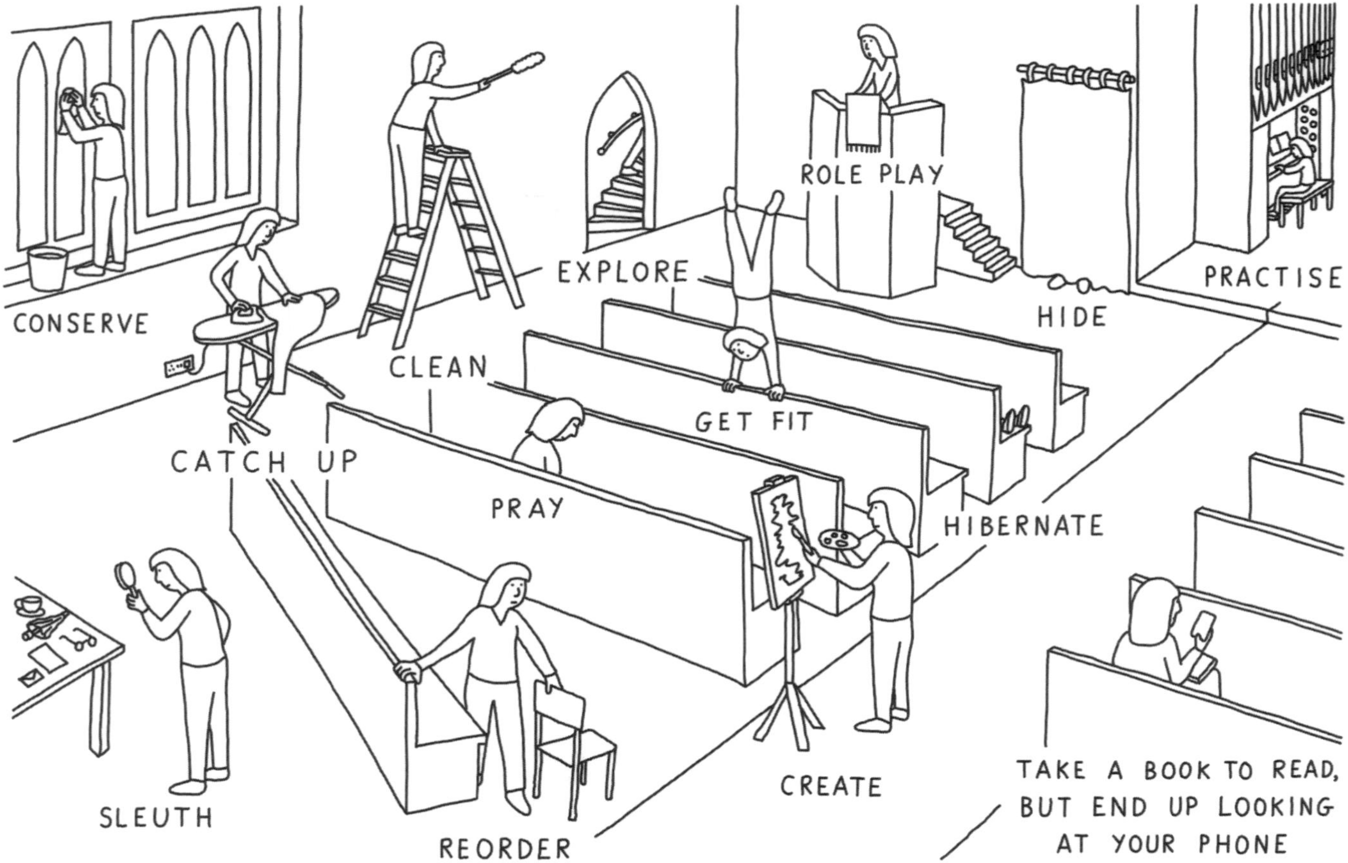

ROLE PLAY
EXPLORE
PRACTISE
HIDE
CONSERVE
CLEAN
GET FIT
CATCH UP
PRAY
HIBERNATE
SLEUTH
REORDER
CREATE
TAKE A BOOK TO READ, BUT END UP LOOKING AT YOUR PHONE

ICE CREAMS

HOW CHURCHGOERS LOOK SIMILAR TO THEIR FAVOURITES

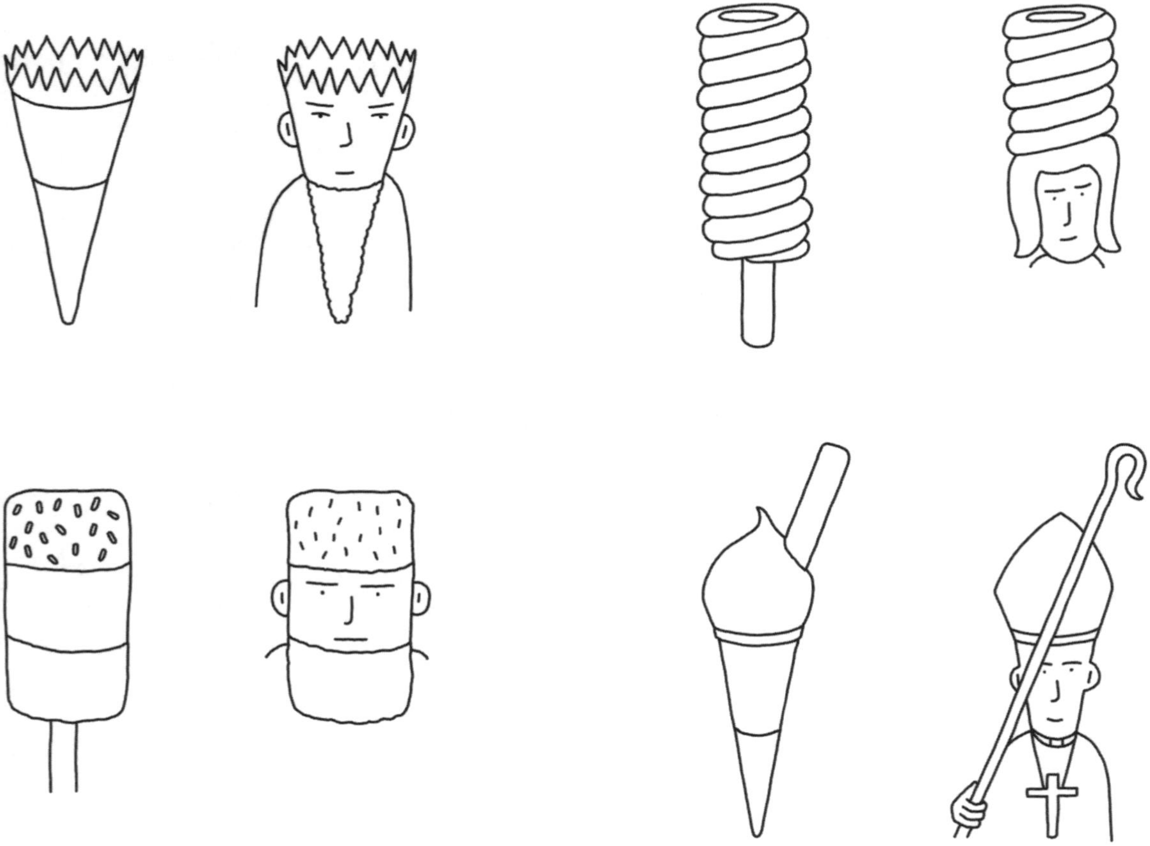

OUTREACH

WE ARE OUTSIDE THE RAILWAY STATION AND WE HAVE SOME PAMPHLETS

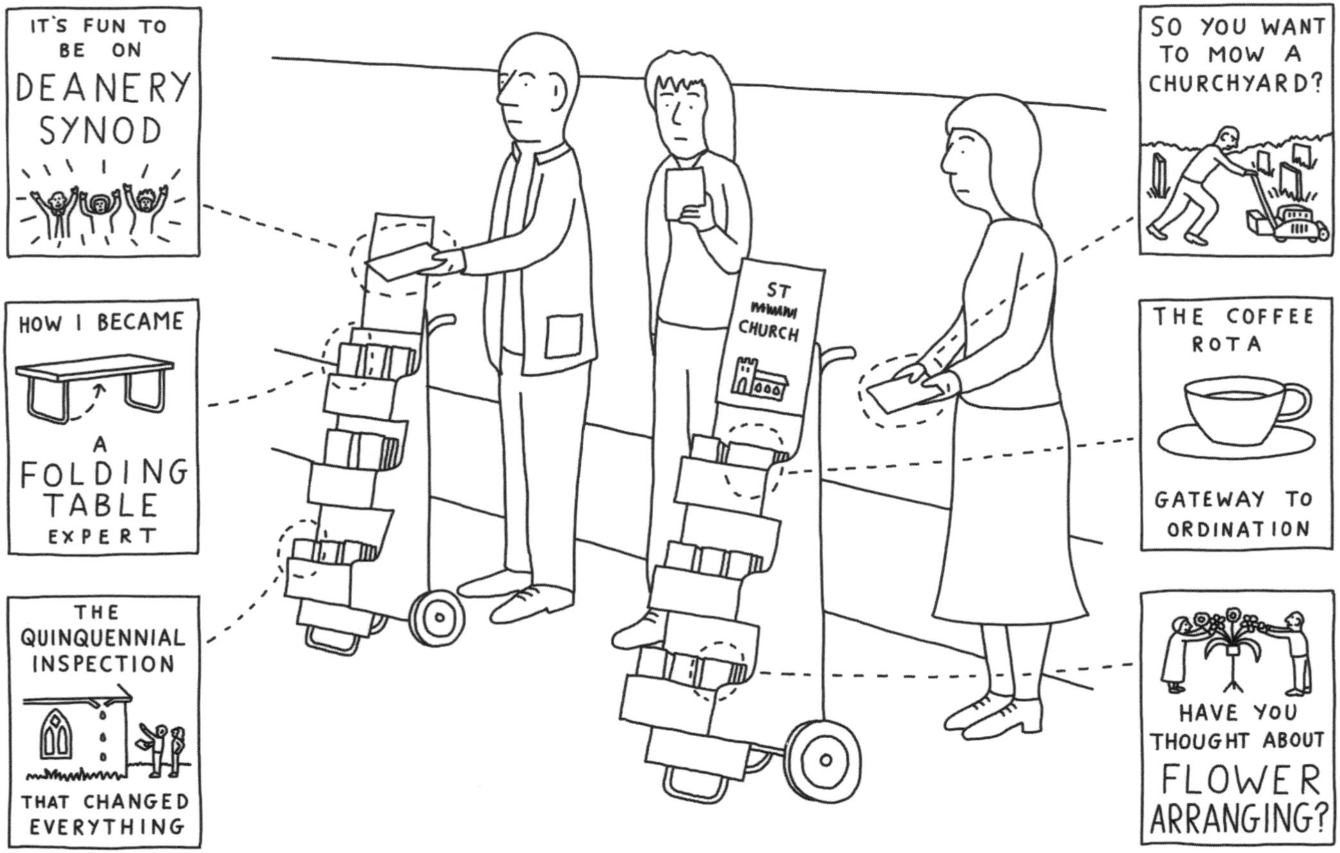
IT'S FUN TO BE ON DEANERY SYNOD
HOW I BECAME A FOLDING TABLE EXPERT
THE QUINQUENNIAL INSPECTION THAT CHANGED EVERYTHING
ST
CHURCH
SO YOU WANT TO MOW A CHURCHYARD?
THE COFFEE ROTA
GATEWAY TO ORDINATION
HAVE YOU THOUGHT ABOUT FLOWER ARRANGING?

VESTMENTS

CARE INSTRUCTIONS

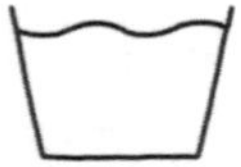

FULL IMMERSION

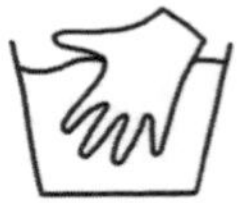

SPRINKLING

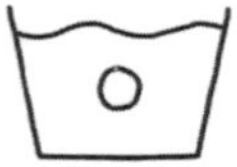

ASK SOMEONE FOR ADVICE

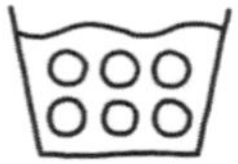

ASK SIX PEOPLE FOR ADVICE

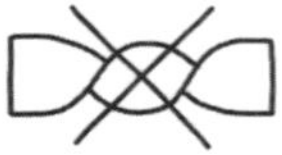

DON'T WEAR AT CHRISTMAS

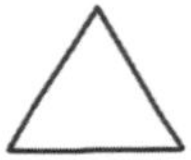

WARNING: YOU'RE PROBABLY GOING TO RUIN IT

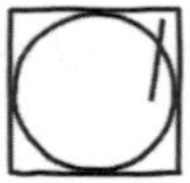

PUT ON SOME LAUNDRY-DAY MUSIC

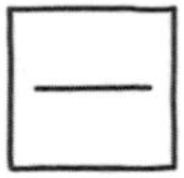

NAP WHILST DRYING

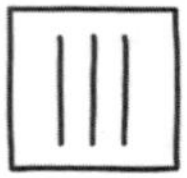

SHOULD BE DRY BEFORE THE CRICKET FINISHES

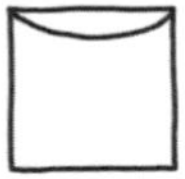

SEALED ENVELOPE IN EXCHANGE FOR LAUNDRY SERVICES

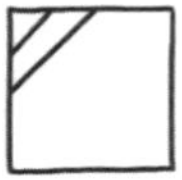

THROW IT IN THE CORNER AND HOPE FOR THE BEST

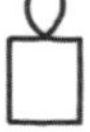

LOOK UP WAX-REMOVAL ADVICE ONLINE

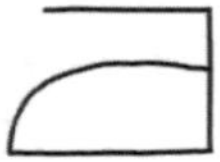

DO I NEED TO IRON THIS?

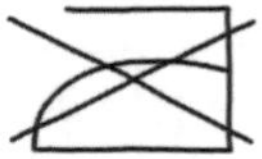

NO, I THINK YOU'RE FINE

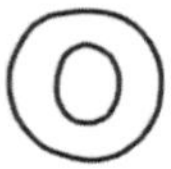
O

DRY CLEAN (ORDINARY TIME)

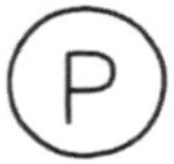
P

DRY CLEAN (PENTECOST)

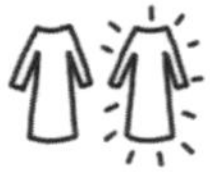

SEPARATE ADVENT AND EASTER BEFORE WASHING

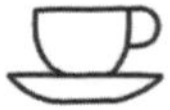

TRY NOT TO SPILL TEA ON IT

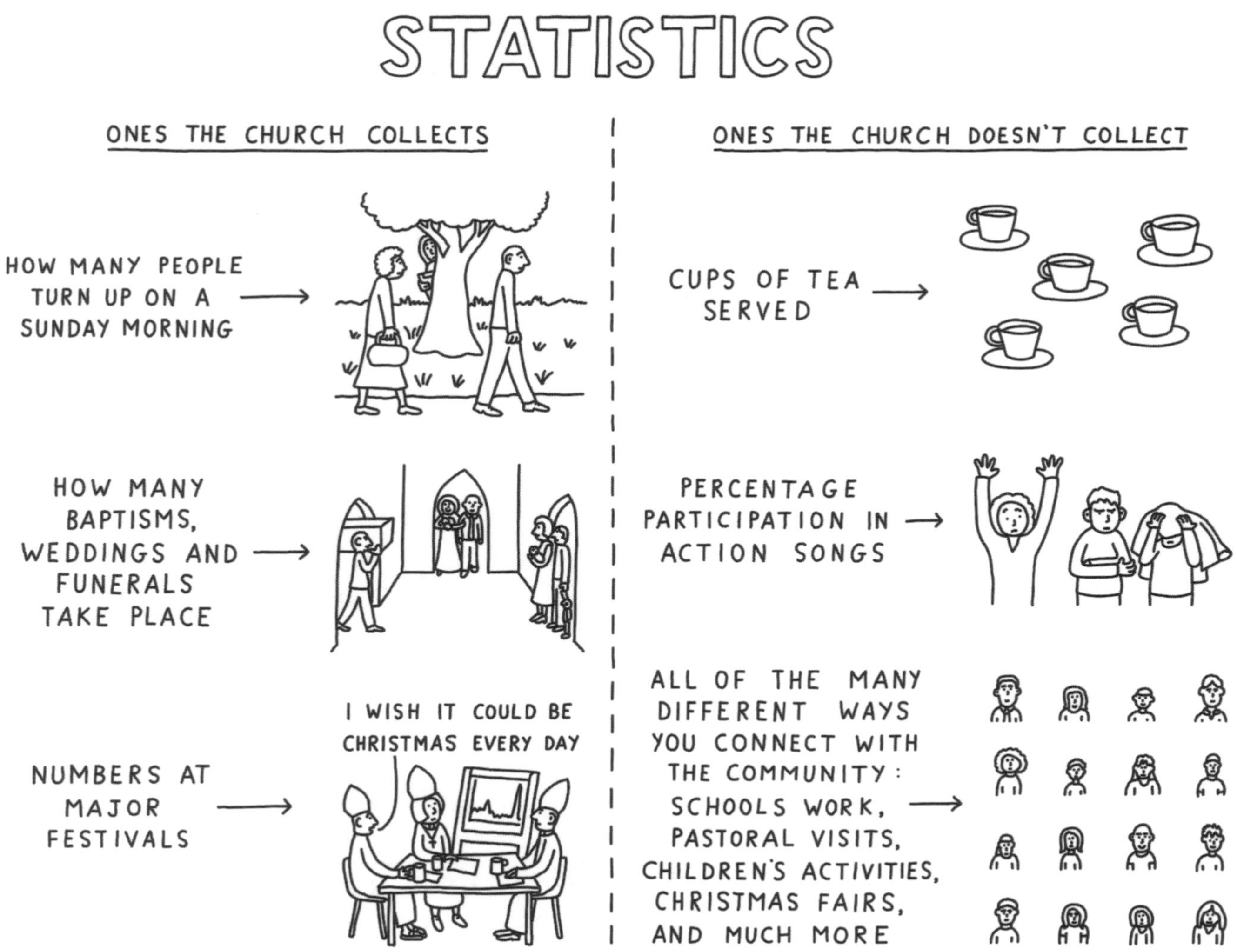

STATISTICS

ONES THE CHURCH COLLECTS

HOW MANY PEOPLE TURN UP ON A SUNDAY MORNING →

HOW MANY BAPTISMS, WEDDINGS AND FUNERALS TAKE PLACE →

I WISH IT COULD BE CHRISTMAS EVERY DAY

NUMBERS AT MAJOR FESTIVALS →

ONES THE CHURCH DOESN'T COLLECT

CUPS OF TEA SERVED →

PERCENTAGE PARTICIPATION IN ACTION SONGS →

ALL OF THE MANY DIFFERENT WAYS YOU CONNECT WITH THE COMMUNITY: SCHOOLS WORK, PASTORAL VISITS, CHILDREN'S ACTIVITIES, CHRISTMAS FAIRS, AND MUCH MORE →
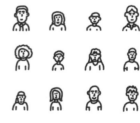

RURAL CHURCHES

WAYS TO USE THEM AND KEEP THEM GOING

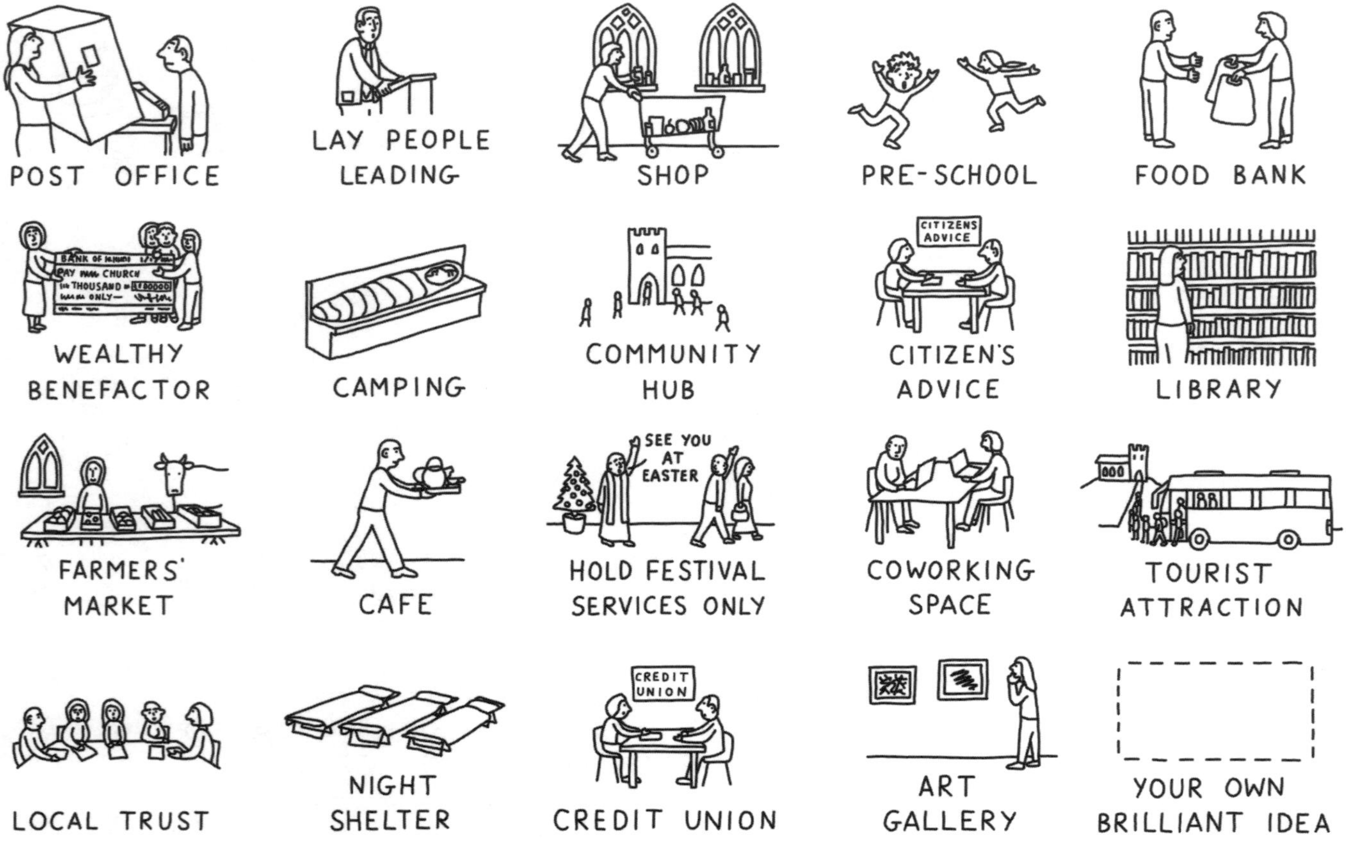

POST OFFICE
LAY PEOPLE LEADING
SHOP
PRE-SCHOOL
FOOD BANK
WEALTHY BENEFACTOR
CAMPING
COMMUNITY HUB
CITIZENS ADVICE
CITIZEN'S ADVICE
LIBRARY
FARMERS' MARKET
CAFE
SEE YOU AT EASTER
HOLD FESTIVAL SERVICES ONLY
COWORKING SPACE
TOURIST ATTRACTION
LOCAL TRUST
NIGHT SHELTER
CREDIT UNION
CREDIT UNION
ART GALLERY
YOUR OWN BRILLIANT IDEA

NEWCOMERS

HOW TO GIVE CHURCH A TRY WITHOUT DETECTION

EVADE THE WELCOMERS

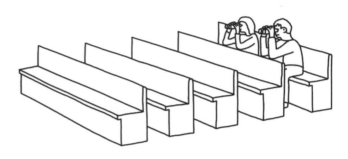

SIT NEAR THE BACK

TRY TO BLEND IN

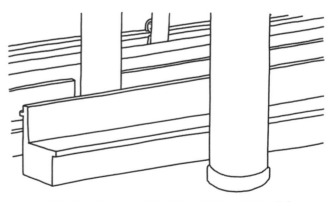

MAKE FULL USE OF THE PILLARS

CHURCH MEMBERSHIP

THE BENEFITS

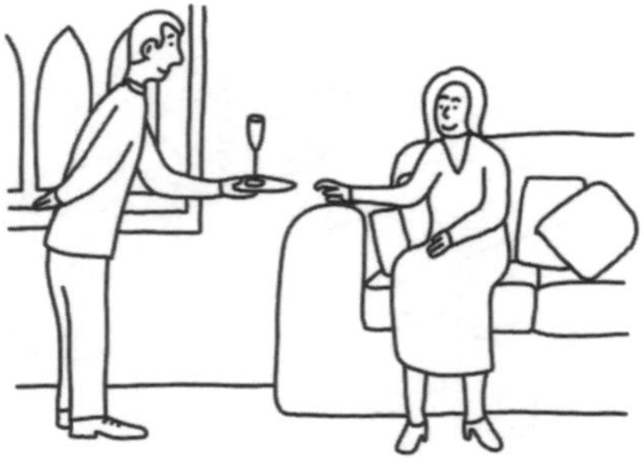

USE OF THE SECRET MEMBERS-ONLY LOUNGE

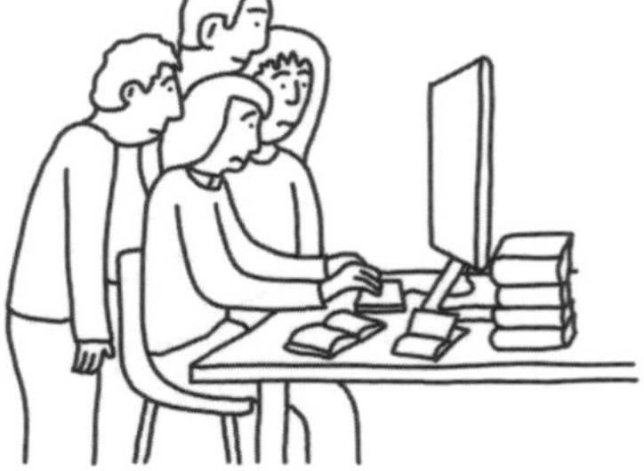

PREVIEWS OF SERMONS THE NIGHT BEFORE RELEASE

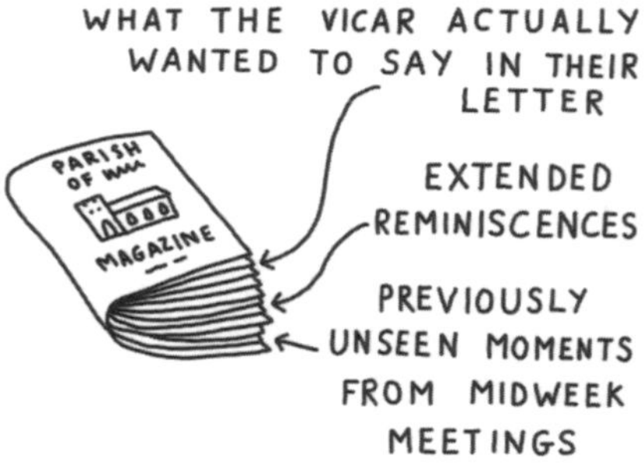
PARISH OF
MAGAZINE
WHAT THE VICAR ACTUALLY WANTED TO SAY IN THEIR LETTER
EXTENDED REMINISCENCES
PREVIOUSLY UNSEEN MOMENTS FROM MIDWEEK MEETINGS

A SPECIAL BUMPER EDITION OF THE PARISH MAGAZINE

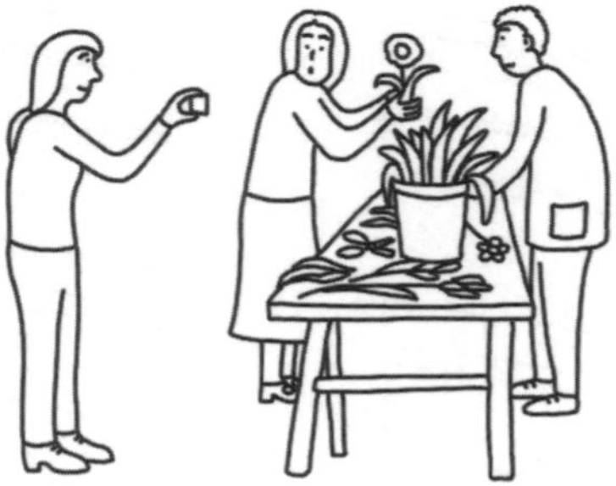

A 'GET OUT OF A ROTA FREE' CARD

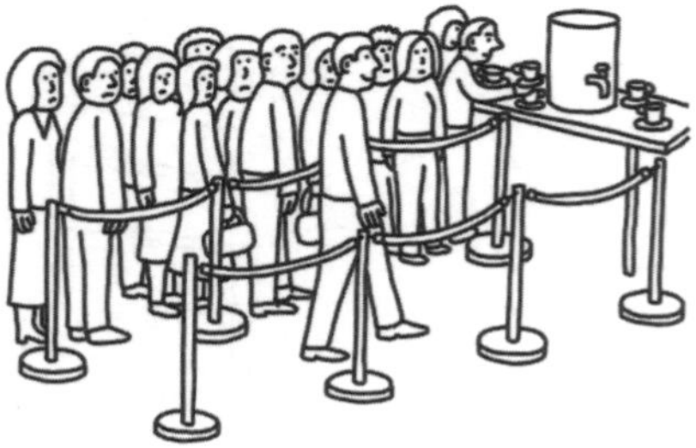

PRIORITY LANE AT AFTER-SERVICE COFFEE

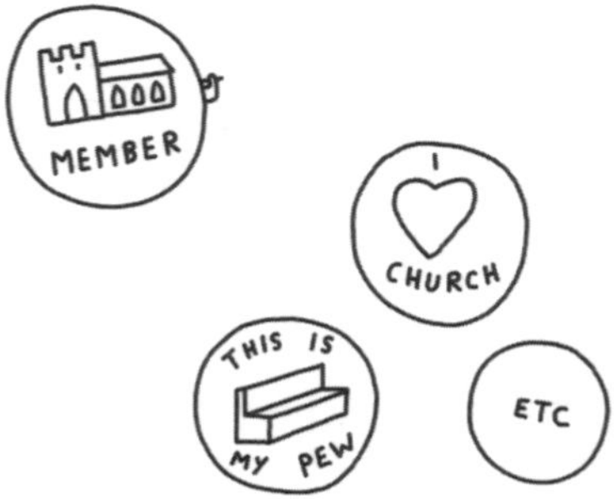
MEMBER
I
CHURCH
THIS IS
MY PEW
ETC

A BADGE, AND SOME STICKERS

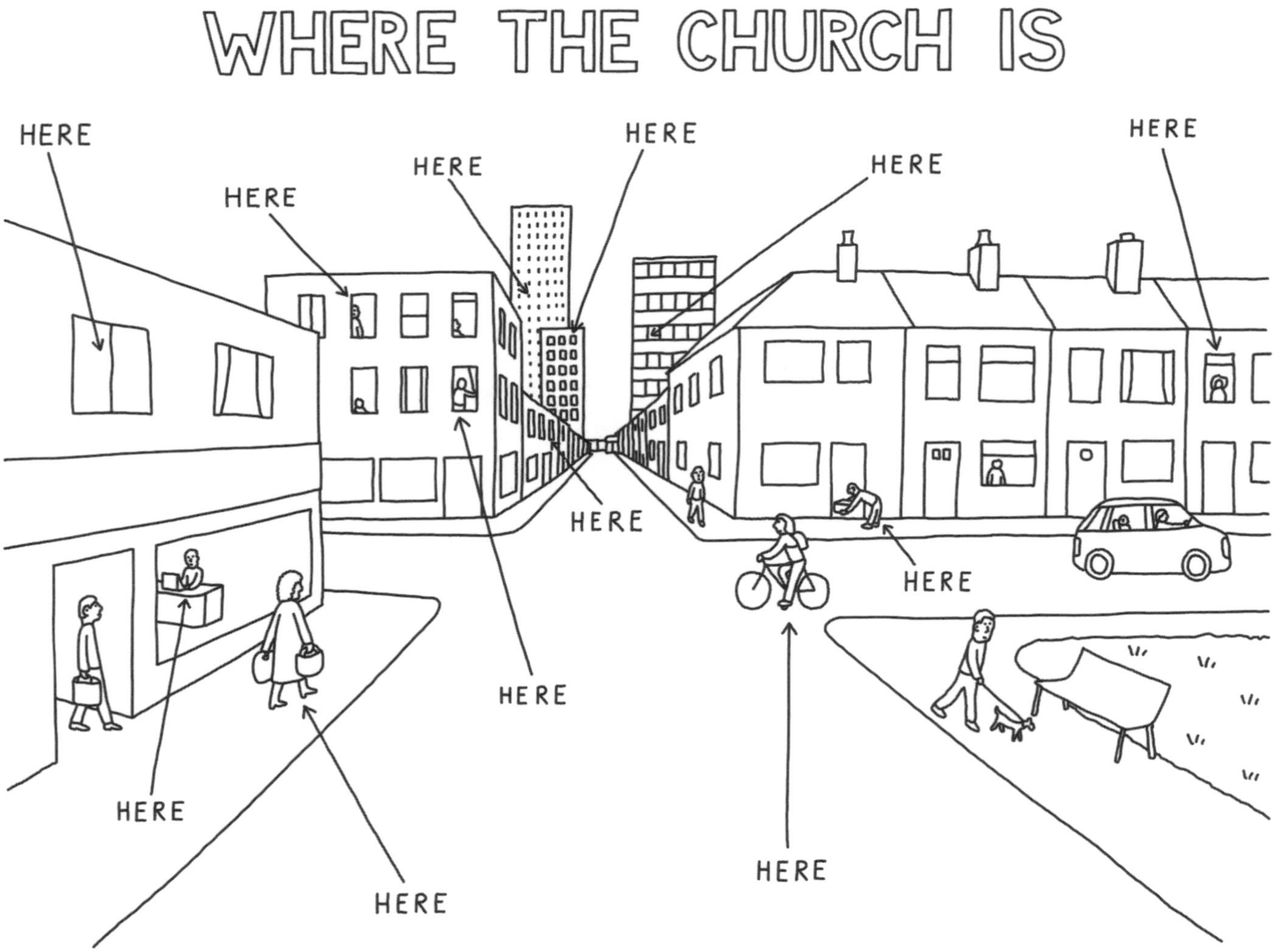
WHERE THE CHURCH IS
HERE
HERE
HERE
HERE
HERE
HERE
HERE
HERE
HERE
HERE
HERE
HERE
HERE
HERE